MAKE IT AND SELL IT

Loretta Holz

MAKE IT AND SELL IT

A Young People's Guide to Marketing Crafts

Photographs by the Author

CHARLES SCRIBNER'S SONS   NEW YORK

Copyright © 1978 Loretta Holz

Library of Congress Cataloging in Publication Data
Holz, Loretta.
Make it and sell it.
Bibliography: p. 135
Includes index.
SUMMARY: Discusses what to make, working with a
group, setting prices, advertising, selling on your
own or through stores, flea markets, and legal information.
1. Handicraft—Marketing—Juvenile literature.
2. Selling—Handicraft—Juvenile literature.
3. Handicraft—Cooperative marketing—Juvenile literature. [1. Handicraft—Marketing. 2. Selling—Handi-
craft] I. Title.
HD2341.H64   658.89′7455   78-1271
ISBN 0-684-15563-X

Three photographs are used courtesy of
Creative Crafts Magazine.

1 3 5 7 9 11 13 15 17 19 V/C 20 18 16 14 12 10 8 6 4 2

Printed in the United States of America

To Kathryn Hudson,
our "Aunt Dot" in Arizona

Contents

Acknowledgments

IN the course of four years of investigating the ways people sell their handcrafted items, I have met and talked to hundreds of crafters of all ages, from young people to senior citizens. These creative people have generously shared their thoughts and suggestions, and I wish to express my gratitude to all of them although I cannot do so by name.

Also I want to thank my editor at Scribners, Clare Costello, for her help and encouragement. Thanks also to Sybil Harp, editor of *Creative Crafts* magazine, who first encouraged me in my investigation of crafts marketing and who continues to do so. Thanks to Wayne Nelson, my local General Business Services representative, who helped with the tax questions. Many thanks also to my mother for her generous typing help.

Foreword

CRAFTS started to become popular in the late 1960's and ever since they have been growing in popularity. People of all ages have been developing a greater interest in creating with their hands.

Young people especially have become more involved in expressing themselves through crafts. In greater numbers they are using their leisure time to learn new crafts and to work with their hands to create beautiful and useful objects for themselves and for others.

Once these young people have mastered a craft, some turn to selling their work in order to be able to continue. Selling not only provides an outlet for their creative productions, it gives them the money they need to buy more materials and equipment in order to experiment further. Moreover, the selling process is interesting in itself and often enjoyable.

If you are one of the growing number of young people who have already started to sell handcrafted items or if you would like to join them, this book is for you. Even if you have never made things before, this book is for you, because it will tell you how to get started in a craft and then how to sell your work.

Perhaps you have been wanting to earn money but have found that part-time and summer jobs are hard to get. While you have been hoping to get someone else to hire you, have you thought of hiring yourself? The possibilities for making money through starting and operating your own small business are almost limitless. The real limits are your time, energy, and interest.

If you start your own business, you are self-employed and as such you enjoy the freedom of doing what you want to do, when you want to do it, while you are earning money working as many or as few hours a week as you wish.

You decide what to make and when and how to sell it. This freedom seldom comes with a regular part-time job and it is something that many adults as well as young people would cherish. It allows you to juggle your work schedule around the demands of your family and your school work.

This book aims at helping you to become an entrepreneur—that is, one who organizes, operates, and assumes the risk for a business venture. It explains how businesses in general operate and gives you ideas for operating your own.

Your business venture is making and selling handcrafted items, and it can be small or grow larger, as you wish. You will be both the manufacturer and the salesman. This book should help you to be both, to see the possibilities that are all around you and to take advantage of them.

The first three chapters of this book tell you about working on your own, with a partner, or with a group. The next two help you to decide what to make and how much to charge for your work. Chapter 6 shows you ways of telling people about your business and your products. The next four chapters tell you how to use the most popular sales methods of craftspeople. Chapter 11 discusses some of the legal and tax implications of your business.

The Additional Information section at the back of the book includes a glossary of business terms, a list of shops where you might sell your work, a list of books you can use to learn a craft, and a list of magazines from which you can find out about shows.

Making and selling your own products can be challenging, profitable, and exciting. If you are willing to work hard at your business, it will give you satisfaction and enjoyment.

ONE

Why Start Your Own Business?

No matter what you will make and no matter how you will sell it, before you start your business give some thought to your *reasons* for doing it. What are your goals? How will you profit from the experience? Is your only aim to earn money?

Earning Extra Dollars

You can earn a few pennies or thousands of dollars or some figure in between, depending on what you make, how many you make, and how you sell your work. But don't be in business only for the money. Your business should be something you enjoy doing; the money is only an added attraction.

Before making money you will probably have to invest "seed money" or initial capital in your project. You'll need materials and equipment and may have to pay for lessons.

Most crafts do not require a large investment. For some, however, a large piece of equipment is needed, like a kiln for pottery. Try to arrange to pay to use someone else's equipment while you experiment making your products and selling them. Once you have tasted success and know that you will continue with your craft, then invest in your own expensive piece of equipment. Perhaps by that time you will have earned enough by selling your work to pay for it. If you don't have the amount you need to start your business, perhaps you can borrow from your parents and pay it back from your first earnings.

Once your project gets underway, you should look on your earnings as working capital, money which you reinvest in materials and whatever else you need. As earnings grow, you should be able to take out some money as payment for your labor.

At the beginning expect to make very little money. Be patient with yourself and your business; you may have to make some false starts before you find the right project and the right market. If you are very lucky, you might find a good item to make right away and do well selling it. Give yourself plenty of time to learn before you become concerned about how much you are earning.

Remember, you're engaged in an enterprise activity. In theory there is no limit as to how far you can go with it or how much you can earn. In contrast, no matter how hard you work as an employee paid at a per hour rate, no matter how creative or efficient you are at doing the job, your earnings are limited to your salary.

Learning About Business

While earning money may be your first goal, it is only one of several you will have in starting your business. Another is to learn just how businesses are started and operated. When you are finished school, there is a good chance you will get a job in a manufacturing or retail business or even run a business of your own. You can learn about being in business by reading a book like this and/or by taking business courses, but you can learn much more and get practical experience by trying it yourself, by seeing what it is really like to run a business if only on a small scale.

You will learn both from your successes and your failures. If things do not go well for you on a project, don't give up. Try to figure out what went wrong and avoid this mistake in the future.

Constantly analyze your projects and activities to find the defects, but don't waste energy worrying about them. Instead immediately plan how to change them in order to correct the problems.

Learning from your mistakes is very important. Any businessperson will tell you that you can't be right all of the time, but you can avoid making the same mistake twice.

Taking Responsibility

If you decide to go into business on your own, selling your handmade items, you will be your own boss, responsible for your own business activities. You must be a self-starter and develop the initiative to see what needs to be done and to do it. You cannot wait for someone else to tell you to get busy and what to do next. You must figure out what you are going to make and look for opportunities to sell your work. To be really successful, create opportunities for yourself whenever possible.

The quality you need to develop is assertiveness. It involves doing what must be done and speaking to those who need to be convinced. It also includes trying out new ideas and defending them when necessary. It means not being afraid to talk to someone, especially someone in authority. And of course your assertiveness must be tempered with consideration, politeness, tact, and purposefulness; if it is, your chances for success are very good.

You also need determination. While you will enjoy your business much of the time, you will also have to take responsibility for tasks that you do not enjoy. If you don't like working with numbers, for instance, you may not like to spend time adding up costs and totaling sales. But you must do this math in order to find out how your business is doing. Or if you have an order for many copies of the same item, you may get tired of doing the same thing over and over and be sorry you took such a large order. But you can't stop and vary your work because you have taken on the responsibility for doing this job and the delivery date is close. You will have to force yourself to work hard and get the order ready.

Planning Your Time

Since you are in business for yourself, you are free to work when you want to and when other activities permit, but you must be disciplined enough to set up a schedule and follow it. Remember that during the school year you must have time for homework plus perhaps club meetings, music lessons, and sporting events.

Once your business gets moving you will have deadlines to meet. If you are going to exhibit in a show, you must have your items made so that they will be ready to sell on the day of the show. If you have promised to deliver an order to a shop, you must have the items ready the day you promised. Don't commit yourself to more orders than you can comfortably handle.

Crafts can be profitable as well as fun. Here David Howitt of Westwood, Massachusetts, makes sand candles.

In order to have your items done on time, set up a schedule and discipline yourself to keep to the schedule as closely as possible. Write down orders and due dates. If you receive a large order from a store, look at your schedule to see how much time you will have to work on the project. If you have four weeks to make three dozen stuffed toys, then plan to have a dozen made at the end of each week. If all goes well the order should be ready a week ahead of time. If you cannot do as much as you expect during any one week, then you will have one last week in which to finish the order.

Building Your Reputation

One of the most valuable assets a businessperson can have is a good reputation. As a businessperson, build a good reputation so that people will buy from you, confident that your products are good and that you will have them ready when promised. Keep your good reputation by playing it straight with everyone—your customers, your suppliers, and your parents. Be loyal to them. Integrity is very important.

As far as your products are concerned, do a good job making them. They may not be the best of all possible items, but they should be the best you can make. If you have done your best, then you should be giving everyone his or her money's worth and perhaps a little more. The fact that you care about your work and how your products look is important to you as a person. The products represent you and you should feel inside that you are doing a good job.

Try to be realistic about what you accomplish. If you are very busy, decide exactly how much time you will have to give to your business so that you will not cheat in any other area of your life including relaxing and having fun. Don't let the job get too demanding and take too much of your time and energy. Remember that your business is only part of your life. It may grow to be the most exciting and enjoyable part, but it is still only a part of the responsibilities you have.

Learning to Make Decisions

Decision making is an important process and since all of your life you will be called on to do it, get experience doing it now in running your own business.

You need facts on which to base a wise decision. Learn to ask the right questions. Go for help to those who can give you the answers.

Keep all of the information organized and ready to use when you need to make a decision. Find a place to keep all of your records, show announcements, sales slips, etc. A looseleaf notebook, a group of file folders, or a small file box might be the answer. If you put all of the papers relating to your business in one place, you should have the information you need when you need it.

Learn to be decisive. Once you have the facts, make up your mind and act on your decisions. Almost every day that you are working on your project, you will have to make decisions. Every businessperson must make them, and some of them turn out to be wrong. If you find that you have made a poor decision, learn from the mistake. Don't "second guess," that is, keep saying to yourself, "if only I hadn't done this." Instead figure out what your mistake was and be ready next time to make a better decision.

Career Experience

When you are applying for a job, one of the most important blanks in the form which you must fill out is "Previous

Experience." If you have something to write in this space you are far ahead of other applicants who have never had any work experience.

If you have successfully made items and sold them, you can write in this space that you were "self-employed." If you can tell your prospective employer about the business you created for yourself and how you ran it, he or she may be very impressed with you. The qualities it takes to start and run a business—initiative, hard work, and determination—are probably what he or she is looking for in an employee.

When you finish school you will have to start supporting yourself. Teachers and guidance counselors and parents have probably made suggestions to you about your career. Many students have a difficult time selecting a career because they don't know what a particular job involves. What does a store manager do all day, or a public relations person, or an accountant? Once you start your business you will learn about a variety of jobs. You'll have the opportunity to meet and talk to people in different lines of work. This practical experience may help you discover what type of career you would like. You might even find that your craft business has developed into a full-time career.

A Growing Business

You have the opportunity to get ahead if you work hard at your business. Many big companies today, especially those involved in making and selling craft supplies, started out small with just one or two products. They grew and developed because the people who started them worked hard to develop the business.

Your business could grow in different ways—ways you could not even predict right now. You might start out

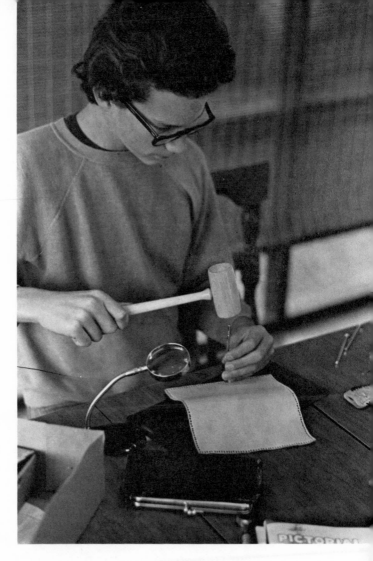

This young leatherworker used a kit, books, and magazine articles to teach himself a craft.

making a variety of different items from wood, for instance, and later find that your best sellers are wooden toys. You might then develop your own wooden toy business and later employ other people as the business grows.

If your lifetime career takes a different direction, as it probably will, after you have finished school and gotten a full-time job, your craft business can still be an enjoyable part-time enterprise, something you do on weekends and in your spare time to unwind from the pressures of your full-time job.

TWO

How About a Partnership?

WHILE you could start out on your own, you might prefer to go into business with someone else. Of course, the first step is to find someone who would like to work with you, your brother or sister, perhaps, or a good friend.

Choose your partner carefully. It is important that you get along well and work well together. Find someone whose talents complement yours, someone whom you genuinely like and don't usually argue with, someone with whom you would like to spend your time. Remember, if your business is a success, you will be spending a lot of time working with your partner. With the right person, your partnership may work very well.

People often set up partnerships because they want to share the responsibility for a project and pool their talents. Often one person is good at one aspect of the job, while the other person is good at another part of the work. For example, you might be very good at thinking up and designing new projects. Your partner, on the other hand, might be good at keeping financial records, while you dislike this aspect of the job. This partnership should work very well. You can design the items, both of you can make them and sell them together, and your partner can keep all of the financial records.

People often set up a partnership to pool their resources. You and your partner will probably each bring some materials and equipment into the partnership, and this will help you to save money. Each of you might have sources of supply for certain kinds of material. With each person supplying materials, your expenses will be lower.

Another advantage to a partnership is that there are two people to talk over problems and come to a decision together. One person may not think of everything that should be taken into consideration. Two together might make a better decision. Moreover, there are two to share the work. If one is busy or sick or on vacation, the other can fill in until the first partner can get back to work. If you must rush on a project, two people can work much faster than one. And some jobs simply require more than two hands!

Companionship is important, too. As you work on a project you can talk and the job will go faster and seem like more fun. The first time you take your work to a store to try to sell it, you can give each other moral support. At a show it is good to have two people to run the booth.

You should be aware, too, of the disadvantages in working with a partner. One of you may be good at one job, the other good at a second job; what about the jobs which neither is good at and neither wants? You must agree to share these or trouble is brewing.

While you have the advantage of two people helping each other to come to a good decision, there will be times when you will disagree. Then who will make the decision? Who will get his or her way? Who will give in?

While there are two people to share the work, what if one partner becomes lazy and lets the other do most of

the work? While companionship is great, what if you begin
to argue?

Learning to Cooperate

If a partnership is to be successful, you must learn to cooperate. Learning to give a little and take a little is an important lesson. If there are jobs that neither of you likes or
is especially good at, figure out how to share the work.
Take turns doing the job or each do part of it.

If you disagree on an important decision, try talking
about it without arguing to see if one partner can convince
the other. If this doesn't work, try to arrive at a mutual
agreement to let one partner make the decision this time,
with the understanding that the other partner should
make the next disputed decision.

To avoid trouble later, put your partnership agreement
in writing. Talk to others in business, think over what
needs to be done, and decide who will do what in your
partnership. If you put the decisions in writing, you cannot disagree later on what you both agreed to do. Of
course, you can make changes in your agreement later as
circumstances change.

Sharing Work, Sharing Profits

Partners should be willing to give equally to their project.
When the partnership is working well, no one needs to
keep track of who is contributing how much time, which
materials, etc. If one partner is slacking off, however, and
not contributing his or her share, something will have to
be done.

Partners should be honest with each other. If you feel

you are contributing more than your share, tell your partner so, but remember that your approach is important. Use the most positive terms possible so that your partner will not get angry but instead will be willing to talk. Discuss problems so that each of you will be free to give your best to the project. Hard feelings and resentfulness can stop anyone from giving what he or she could to a partnership.

If one partner simply cannot give as much as the other, then the partners might be able to work out an agreement to change the percentage of how much each contributes and how much each gets in profits. The partner who does the major share of the work might get 75% of the profits while the partner who cannot contribute as much might get only 25%.

THREE

Working with a Group

WHILE you can do many projects alone or with a partner, you can become involved in much more exciting ventures if you have a whole group of people to work on the project. The group might be fellow students at school or members of a club or some of your neighborhood friends. Each person may be earning spending money or you may be raising money as a group for a specific cause, perhaps a class trip.

Working with a group on a project can have many advantages. Members can pool their talents. Those who have artistic ability can design the items to be made, those who like to deal with people can be the salespeople, and those who are good at math can do the accounting.

A group can take on a much larger project than an individual or two partners because there are so many hands to help and jobs can be done quickly. Working with a group can be fun, and if you do well you can enjoy success together. Another advantage is that if many people are running the business, you can break down the work in much the same way a manufacturer does and thus get some idea of how a business operates.

On the other hand, members of a group sometimes disagree on what is to be done and nothing significant is accomplished. If some are uncooperative, the whole group will suffer.

Method of Operation

Your group could organize itself in many different ways. Much will depend on whether you are working on a short-term or long-term project, whether you are earning money for a common cause or for each individual, and whether the group members will work together on all aspects of making and selling.

You might make the items together and sell them separately. After learning the craft and making the items together, each one of your group could then sell his or her own items through stores, shows, his own sale, or by calling on friends in their homes. (All of these methods of sale are discussed in Chapters 7–10.)

Another alternative is to make the items by yourselves and then get together to do the selling. You might each be producing the same items or, more likely, each one would be working on his own different craft.

Making Together, Selling Together

If you decide to make your items together and sell them together as well, your group could set up its own company. By doing this you could learn much about how a business operates.

The first step in setting up your business might be to get an adult sponsor to help you with the project. The group will need a place to meet and to work, so perhaps you have already chosen your sponsor who will allow you to work in his or her home or classroom. If it is a neighborhood group perhaps one of the parents might be willing to be the sponsor, especially if the group hopes to use this parent's basement as the "factory."

If you are working with a group of fellow students, perhaps a teacher would sponsor your project. If you are learning crafts through a school program, perhaps the teacher in charge of the program would help you with the project and get permission for you to use the classroom as your "factory." Or perhaps your social studies teacher would let you turn your "company" into a class project.

Getting Organized

The first step is to call a meeting of all who might be interested in your project. Probably the nucleus or small group of students or friends who have come up with the idea will be the first members of the group. In turn, they might urge their friends to come to the first meeting.

At the meeting those who have proposed the idea could tell everyone what they have in mind and hear opinions and suggestions. Who will be the sponsor? What will you make? How can you sell it? Where can you work? Who will run the business? You will probably need to have several planning meetings. Questions raised at one meeting could be investigated by members between meetings so that perhaps at the next gathering a decision could be made.

The group could be run as a cooperative, with each person having one vote. The members would have to meet perhaps once a month and more often at the beginning. At one of the first meetings select a name for your business. Let everyone make suggestions and then vote. Try to find something clever so people can easily remember the name. Also try to have the name tell something about your business and the type of products you will sell.

Look for a symbol, insignia, or logo by which your group can be known. Again, everyone might be encouraged to try to work up designs and from those submitted the members could choose the one to be used. Both the name and the symbol could be used on labels for your products.

Rules of Operation

Once you decide that your group wants to have its own business, establish some rules. Even if all of the members are friends and get along well with one another, ground rules are a good idea to insure that everything will continue to go well. Of course anyone who refuses to follow the rules will drop out of the group.

Write up the rules of operation as a "constitution." A few volunteers might form a committee to develop the constitution. Once they have a tentative one, the membership could discuss it, make any necessary changes, and then vote to accept it. Any members who join after the constitution is adopted should receive a copy and agree to its provisions before accepting membership.

The constitution should answer such questions as: How does a new member join the group? When will the business meetings be held? What officers will the group have? What duties will they have? How will they be elected? How long will they hold office? What must a member do in order to continue his or her membership?

What happens if a member must be dropped?

Before writing the constitution decide at a very early meeting what officers you need and the duties of each. Elect a president, who will oversee the whole operation and be in charge of the group meetings. Important decisions will be voted on by the whole group, but the president should have the power to make decisions when the group cannot meet. Elect a secretary to take notes at the meetings and do the necessary correspondence and a treasurer to handle the company's funds and do all of the accounting.

The work that must be done within the company might be divided into phases. The first is management and that would be handled by the officers as a group. For each of the remaining phases elect an officer in charge.

Your director of research and development, along with his or her staff, would figure out what products the group should make and arrange to have samples made. The production director or manager would be in charge of the actual making of the items. The purchasing agent or the production director would order materials. The sales manager would be in charge of selling. Publicity could be handled by the sales manager or by a separate officer. A membership chairperson or personnel officer could deal with those who want to become new members of the group.

All officers in charge of specific phases of the business, along with the president, secretary, and treasurer, could form the executive board which would meet between the general meetings and plan for them as well as for the company in general. The board might have power to make certain decisions while others would have to be voted on by all the members.

Being a part of the company should be a learning experience for everyone so the group might vote to change jobs fairly frequently and give all members a chance to see what the various officers do. Everyone will of course be involved in production, even the president. All members should be encouraged to get involved in as many other aspects of the company as possible so that they learn as much as possible about running a company.

Selling Stock

Before starting your business, you need capital. The old cliche "you must have money to make money" is quite true. You will need to invest in equipment and materials before you can start production.

The money you need at the beginning of your venture is called the initial capital. When you start your own business, you might have some of this initial capital yourself. If not, you must borrow from friends or relatives.

Another alternative is to find a "venture capital" group or company which specializes in lending money to start businesses and in return owns part of the new business. Do you know anyone who would like to invest in your company?

Your group must decide where to get their initial capital. You and your friends might each be able to give some money, collecting it in an organized and fair manner. A good procedure is to sell "stocks" in your company. These can be handprinted papers that say the owner has one or more shares.

First decide how much money is necessary to buy materials and equipment and to cover other start-up costs. Then calculate how many shares of stock to sell and how much each one should cost. You might decide to print up a hundred shares of stock and sell each for a dollar in order to have a hundred dollars to start your project.

Decide who can buy stock. Your group might want to limit sales to members with each one allowed to buy only a certain number. On the other hand, you might decide that each person *must* buy a certain number. The group might also decide to sell shares to non-members. Be sure to keep a list of stockholders, noting beside each name how many shares of stock that person has.

The money collected from selling the stock would be used by your company as working capital. Some large and prosperous companies give each stockholder a dividend, a certain amount of money each year depending on how many shares of stock that person holds. If your company is in business a long time you could declare a dividend and pay each stockholder an amount on each share he or she owns.

A company that goes out of business is usually bankrupt and its stockholders therefore lose out. They can lose all the money they invested in the company or receive back only part of it.

If on the other hand when you vote to go out of business, your company still has money after debts and salaries have been paid, the stockholders should get back the money they invested together with profit on their investment.

How Will You Be Paid?

If you are all working to make money for a specific cause, there is no problem about distributing the money. If, however, you are each working for pocket money for yourselves, you must figure out a fair and easy way to distribute the money which the company makes. Members of your group could all be considered "employees" of your company.

Two different ways are used to pay employees. Those who are paid higher wages, usually the executives of a company and those who hold management or research jobs, are paid an annual salary. No matter how many hours they must spend working to do their job properly, they receive the same amount of money. Other workers, like those who work on assembly lines or who do clerical work, are usually paid by the hour. If they work more hours than the usual number in a specific week they are paid "overtime."

You could set up your method of payment either way. Everyone could be "on salary" and each one would receive the same amount of money as long as he or she worked a certain number of hours. Everyone would have to give at least the minimum time needed to run the business.

If the group decides instead to pay members at a per hour rate, set up a system of time cards. Each member should have a card on which to write down the time he or she starts to work and the time he or she stops. The accountant or treasurer would use these cards to figure out each person's paycheck.

Producing and Selling

Once your group gets organized you can start production on sample items. Of course you will want to start selling them right away. Your company can choose to sell in different ways. It should be fun, exciting, and profitable to run your own sale as explained in Chapter 8. You could have an outdoor summer show, for example, or an inside event just before Christmas.

Note that for a show you will need lots of items to sell. You really don't want to make up many items, however, until you know that they will be good sellers. Before launching into a big sale, your company might want to test products by having members sell them to friends and relatives to get opinions on them. Sell them door-to-door directly, as explained in Chapter 7, or take a booth at a show, as explained in Chapter 10.

Another way to test your products is to take samples to retail stores as explained in Chapter 9. If the shop manager is willing to buy them outright, you must have a good product. Or he or she might take them on consignment and give them a chance in the shop, paying you only for items that customers buy and returning the unsold items to you.

Once you have found that your products are selling well, your company could launch its own big show, building up to it over a period of time. The show should be well planned and have lots of publicity. Everyone in the company should have a part in it. If the show is a success, the members will be eager to get back to work on more products and prepare for the next sale.

FOUR

What Will You Make?

If you want to start selling what you make, you must first decide what to make. This chapter cannot tell you exactly what you should make, but it can help you to make a good choice. Choose your craft and your products carefully because the craft you pick and the items you decide to make can make your job of selling easy or difficult.

Choosing Your Craft

Perhaps you are already skilled in a craft. If so consider what items you could make to sell. Perhaps you know a craft that is part of your ethnic tradition. If you are of Polish descent, for example, your parents might have taught you to do the traditional paper cutting of Poland. Use this skill to make designs for greeting cards, stationery, or wall decorations.

If you do not already have a craft skill, choose one you

Virginia Norey learned the art of Polish paper cutting from her mother. She often demonstrates her craft at shows and at cultural exhibits.

think you will enjoy. If you don't like the one you chose, change to another. Many people "watch the clock" as they work because they are not enjoying their jobs. You have the opportunity of *choosing* what to make, however, so you should not be a "clock watcher" but one who enjoys working.

If you can draw or paint, choose a craft in which you can use this ability. If you like being outdoors, choose one that uses natural materials which you can find while walking through the woods. If you like to work with fabrics, choose a craft that uses them.

Certain crafts are much better than others for people who want to make money selling their work. Avoid crafts that take a long time to learn, or require very expensive equipment or materials, or are so time-consuming that many hours are needed to make one item.

Even if the first craft you learn is not commercially successful, you did not waste your time; you learned a new technique and now you know better the type of craft you are looking for.

Learning a Craft

Crafts are very popular and there are many ways to learn about them. They are taught in some schools as part of art class. Most high schools and many junior high or middle schools have industrial arts programs which may feature woodworking and other crafts. Some have special after-school programs or mini-courses in crafts. Find out what your school system offers.

Camps, summer schools, YW and YMCA's, and museums often offer craft classes. Some craft supply stores have workshops for adults and children.

Learn from people you know, perhaps even one of your own parents. This would be ideal because right at home you would have the equipment and materials you need to get started. If you know a professional craftsperson, see if he or she is willing to let you be a student "apprentice" and help around the shop while learning the craft.

You can also teach yourself through books and magazines. Check the shelves of your local library and bookstores. (See page 135 for a list of helpful books.)

Once you have learned a craft, look for products to make. If you make a single item and it proves to be popular, you can make just this one item, perhaps using different designs or in different colors.

If the item you choose to make is a fad, don't make a large supply even if it is selling very quickly. You don't know when the fad suddenly will die. While you are mak-

Diane Poli's father taught her the Japanese craft of bonsai, the training of miniature trees. Diane sells her creations at shows and through her family's nursery business.

ing this item, look for other ideas so that you will be ready to switch to a new item when this one is no longer popular.

To increase sales, you may want to make a whole line of items. If you do leather craft you can make belts, wallets, pocketbooks, etc. With a whole line of products you have a better chance to sell to any one customer because he or she will have a greater number of items in a greater price range from which to choose.

What Makes a Good Product?

When you are deciding which specific items or lines of items to make, keep in mind the qualities of a good product: uniqueness, good design, quality workmanship, and customer appeal.

Uniqueness means that your product is different from what other people are selling. As you learn your craft, think about products you could make. Look for ideas in books. See what your teacher and fellow classmates have made. If possible visit a store that sells handmade items and see what is for sale. Try not to copy another person's idea but let original items give you ideas for what you can make.

Uniqueness is important because if you are making the same items as others, your sales will be much less. For example, you might have a booth at a show and be selling necklaces of handmade beads. If you are the only person selling such necklaces you could do quite well, but if there are ten other people selling necklaces of similar quality for a similar price, the number of customers interested in beads must be divided among those making the necklaces. To do better than your competitors in this case, yours would have to be outstanding in quality or design or your prices much lower. But why try to compete when it is much easier to sell an item different from those sold by others?

Good design is also important in any item you make. Design is the first thing customers notice. Only if they like this will they look further at the workmanship, materials, and price. Good workmanship is also important because if your items have dirty spots, dabs of glue, bits of thread hanging, or other evidence of careless, sloppy work, customers will not want them. And the materials are important. Don't waste your work on poor materials. Use the best you can get at a reasonable price.

What Does Your Customer Like?

Think about who will buy your items and try to make things that your typical customer would like. Make items you enjoy working on and ones that you think are beautiful and worthwhile, but keep in mind that if you want to sell your work, you must please your customers.

While people like to buy some decorative items for

their homes and to give as gifts, they have a greater need for useful and practical items. If your products are practical as well as decorative you have a chance for even greater sales.

Ask yourself—will I be selling to adults or people of my own age? Will my customers be male or female? Will they be buying articles for themselves or as gifts? If as gifts, for whom? The answers to these questions will help you to decide what to make.

If you plan to sell to people of different ages, use various designs: some to appeal to children, others to parents or grandparents.

A customer must not only like the items but be willing to pay the price you are asking. Of course, the lower the price the more likely the customer will be to buy. Therefore it's a good idea, at least at first, to make less expensive items. Once your customers know you and your product they will be willing to buy more expensive items.

Market Research

At the beginning you will have only a small number of items to sell because you are testing them to see if customers will be interested in buying them. It is important to test before you decide to build up an inventory, that is, a good supply of completed items ready for sale.

Big companies spend large amounts of money doing "market research," testing their new products before they build up an inventory. First they study the products of their competitors and then they make up samples of their own, offer them to a small number of test customers, and pay close attention to how these customers react. The company wants to find out, first, if people will buy the new item and, second, if customers have complaints about the product. The company wants to improve the product and increase sales.

You will do the same thing, although you may not call what you are doing "market research." See what other craftspeople are selling, make up a small number of samples, and offer them for sale to customers. Pay close attention to what they say, because their suggestions might help you to improve your product. Once you know that a certain item will sell, make up many more.

Custom Work

One of the biggest selling points for your work is the fact that you can make exactly what the customer orders according to his or her desires. It might be a matter of making your item with a requested design, or in another color which the customer prefers. Or you might personalize the item by painting or stitching a person's name.

Perhaps your craft lends itself well to personalizing. If you embroider you can stitch the designs in colors your customer prefers, adding his or her name to the item if desired. You could even do the embroidery right on your customer's shirt or jeans or on whatever other item he or she gives you to decorate.

Perhaps you make rock figures by glueing ordinary rocks together into a standing figure and painting them. You might develop some standard figures: a teacher, a golfer, a tennis player, a housewife, a businessperson, and so on. Customers then could choose which figure they want in the hair color and outfit they wish. If you get a special request and do not have an appropriate figure, develop one especially for this customer and perhaps add this figure to your line.

With some selling methods, custom orders are very

*Embroidery is an attractive
way to personalize an article.
This young craftsperson
is decorating a shirt.*

easy to handle. If you are selling to people you know, you can easily do custom work for them. If you are running your own sale as described in Chapter 8, you can ask customers to come back and pick up their custom orders. Selling through personal visit and through a home party as described in Chapter 7 are methods of sale ideally suited to custom orders.

At a bazaar, show, or flea market, taking special orders would be difficult. Instead try to give your customers the widest range of choice you can by having a variety of items in different colors from which the customer can choose. If you make something that you can personalize quickly while the customer waits, your sales should be good. If you make wall plaques, have them all ready to be sold, leaving room in the corner for a person's name. Paint in the name when the plaque is sold.

If you are selling your work through a shop, the shop manager can take special orders for you. The customer giving the order should be willing to pay a deposit, that is, part of the cost of the item in advance. You would then make up the item, and when the customer picks it up, he or she would pay the remainder.

Getting Materials

If you will be making only a few items, you will have to buy your materials at retail prices, that is, their regular prices in stores. See which local store or which mail order catalog has the lowest prices for good quality materials. Also look for sales and specials. If it will not affect the quality of your product, use "seconds" or "irregulars" which you should be able to buy for half price.

For some crafts you may be buying large amounts of the same material. Try to buy it at wholesale or discount prices if possible. If you are taking lessons, your teacher may help you find a wholesale source. If not, perhaps your local craft shop will give you a special discount on large orders.

Whether you have paid retail or wholesale prices for your materials, use them carefully. Save money by not wasting them and by thinking of uses for scraps you might otherwise throw away.

Will You Be Making Many?

Once you find that a certain item sells well, build up your inventory. Look for ways of working which will make the job easier and quicker.

When a large company wants to make many of the same items, the management usually sets up an assembly line because they find the quickest way to make something is to divide the steps among a number of workers and have each person do the same step over and over again to each object as it is passed to him or her. Often a conveyer belt or moving platform brings the items from one person to the next.

If you are working with a group, set up your own assembly line. If you are making painted wooden toys, for example, one person could saw the wood, the next person sand the items, a third one nail them together, while the last person in the assembly line would paint them. If there is lots of painting to do, several people might paint. Each one could do a certain color or area on the toy. If you are setting up an assembly line, experiment to find the best way to divide the work—and change jobs occasionally so that no one gets tired of a certain job.

Joseph Eng sells his bamboo boats at an outdoor art festival.

Working assembly-line style is helpful when you are making many of the same kind of item. Tracey Reilly of Westfield, New Jersey, cuts a supply of fringe to decorate the puppets she is making.

If you are working by yourself, use the assembly line method by working on a group of items together. If you are making wooden toys, cut out a dozen at once, sand them as a group, and so on. If you must wait between steps, perhaps for the paint to dry, have several groups of items started.

Another possibility is to hire someone to help you. Perhaps you can get your younger brother or sister or a young neighbor to help with some of the easier jobs, like sanding the pieces of wood.

Whether you are working alone or with a group, it is very important to have quality control. This means checking to see that each item is well made and meets the standard of workmanship you want your products to have. Before packing each finished item inspect it, checking it over carefully for flaws.

Your Label

One thing that makes your items interesting to customers is the fact that *you made* them. You are special because you have a craft talent and you have been able to make items that people will buy. The people who buy them— and if they are gifts, the people who receive them—are interested in you and your work. Therefore it is a good idea to attach a label to each item to tell your story.

The label can be just a piece of paper or card, perhaps with a single fold. Use a small drawing to decorate it and then write your story briefly. Print or write the label yourself or type it or have someone type it for you. Make more copies on a copy machine or on a ditto machine, if you know someone who has access to one. If you will be selling many items, you might even get a printer to make copies.

On your label tell who you are and what your craft is. If necessary give simple instructions for using the item. Think about the questions that people have asked you and answer them on the label. Figure 1 shows a simple label— perhaps yours will be similar.

Figure 1

```
              This colorful mobile was made
           especially for you by Jane Murphy,
           a student at Warren Middle School.
    Having taught herself mobile making, Jane
    creatively uses bits of wire, paper and string
    to make original mobiles.
          Hang your attractive new mobile at eye
    level or a little higher where the air or heat
    currents will make its parts move and dance for
    your enjoyment.
```

Setting Prices

ALMOST every beginner in crafts has a hard time deciding on prices. Remember there are two important figures to keep in mind—what you would like to receive for the item and what your customer is willing to pay. If these are close together you have a successful sale.

Basically there are three ways to set prices. The first involves figuring out all of your costs. In order for your business to be profitable you must charge enough to cover all of these plus payment for yourself for the time spent making an item and selling it.

The second method of figuring out prices involves finding out how much customers are willing to pay for your work. If people will not pay your prices, your business will not be successful.

The third method is guessing. This is the way most craftspeople may tell you they set their prices. However, if they are good at setting prices they are really unconsciously using one or probably both of the other methods.

While setting good prices is important as far as making

your business profitable is concerned, don't be overconcerned. Take into consideration what you can, and set a price. If you find that you are not getting enough for an item, change the price. Experiment with prices cautiously, learning what you can from what happens. You are not locked into the first price you set unless you have taken a big order at that price and must fill it without raising the price. Note, however, that regular customers and shop managers may complain when you raise prices.

While at first you might guess at a good price, if you are going to make money with your business, you must keep records and figure out exactly how much you are making on each item. If you are not making enough on a specific item, stop making it and go on to something else more profitable.

How Does a Businessperson Set Prices?

Have you ever looked at the price of an item in a store and said to yourself: I could make this for half the price, or a third, or a fourth, or even less? When you said that, what were you taking into consideration? Were you thinking only of the materials?

When people start making things to sell they often underprice their work because they are only trying to cover the cost of the materials and perhaps get a little more for their labor.

When you set prices, you must think of much more than materials and a little more for labor because if you do not take all expenses into account, you will lose money no matter how much business is done. The figure you end the year with—that is, the total of all sales minus all costs—must come out a plus, that is, a profit, or you will probably go out of business.

Businesspeople often figure out an easy "pricing formula," a quick way to set the price on a specific item. For example, they might discover that for their products the retail price should be about five times the cost of the materials. Once you have worked out the exact price figures for some of the products you make, you might find an easy formula like that which works well for you. In the meantime figure out your actual costs.

Cost of Materials

In order to make anything you need materials. Some you may have right at home, especially if you are using scrap or recycled materials. Perhaps your mother sews and gives you all of the small pieces of material she has left over. Or if you are making wooden items you may be able to use leftover pieces of wood from your father's workshop. But you may soon run out of scraps and will have to buy your materials. Find out how much the materials cost and figure this cost into the price.

If you are using natural materials you must find a source and then gather the acorns, pine cones, or whatever. While natural materials are free, remember you spend time gathering them and you should get paid for your time.

If several sources in your area carry the material you need, comparison shop, that is, see what the same material costs in several different stores. Find out from each what discount you can get when you are ready to buy in larger quantities. Look for the best quality materials at the lowest price.

If your business grows you may be able to buy materials at wholesale, but don't buy a large quantity until you are certain that the product for which you need the material is selling well.

The Yellow Pages may be able to give you a source. Other craftspeople might suggest sources to you. Consider combining your order with that of another craftsperson so that the total order will be large enough to get a discount price.

If you are taking lessons, ask your teacher about materials. Perhaps he or she could sell you materials at a discount price or direct you to a good source.

How Long to Make?

In order to set fair prices you need to know how long it took you to make a specific item. If you are making a large number, make them in groups working as on an assembly line. Don't time yourself until you are working efficiently. Once you are, do a group of items, whatever number is convenient. Count the time it took you from setting up through clean-up. Divide the total amount of time by the number of items and you will know how long it takes per item.

Once you know how long it takes to make a specific item, put a price on your time. Consider how much you would be making per hour if you worked for someone else. Remember that if you went out to work you would lose time getting ready and going to the place where you were working. Your wages would be less, considering the total time spent, than the per hour rate. That is, you might spend six hours earning four hours' worth of wages.

Set your wages fairly low at first, and see how this affects the price of your items. You may have to start out making less than you want to be able to earn. Naturally

Younger brothers and sisters can be hired to sort, pack, and do other useful jobs.

as time goes by your wages should go up quite a bit.

Remember that your business should grow. The longer you are making things, the more skilled you will be and the smarter you will be at finding ways to sell them. At first you will make mistakes and waste time—by going to unprofitable shows, for instance. All of this learning is an investment in the future and part of your business education. As you get more experience, you will be more efficient and successful, and you will be earning more when you base your income on a per-hour rate.

Remember, too, that there are compensations for the low wage you set for yourself. You can work almost whenever you want to, thus using time that might otherwise have been wasted. Sometimes you can even do two things at once, like watching TV while making your items.

The benefits you'll derive from starting and developing your own business should more than outweigh the disadvantage of low wages. The freedom you'll enjoy and the possibility for growth cannot be measured in terms of money.

Overhead

In addition to the cost of materials and labor, people in business must consider many other costs they might have in producing an item. These additional costs, called "overhead," can be thought of as the hidden costs, those you do not usually consider when you are figuring the cost of making a single item.

Overhead costs include rent, insurance, and utilities including electricity, gas, telephone, and water. They also include the office supplies you might need in order to write to suppliers, stores, customers, etc. Any special equipment you had to buy in order to be able to make your items is also part of the overhead, as is the designing time, that is, the time you took to plan and make models of the items you are producing.

Businesses usually add a percentage to their other costs in order to cover overhead. For example, they might use a formula that adds one-third of the cost of the labor for overhead. Your overhead of course will not be as high as someone who rents a factory but you do have some of the other costs mentioned above.

If you use quite a bit of electricity for your craft, then you should be giving your parents money to help pay their higher utility bill. You might add a few cents to the cost of each item you sell to cover your overhead expenses.

Selling Costs

When you have added up the cost of the materials, labor, and overhead you have only half of the cost of the item—that is, the manufacturing half. The cost of any product you buy must be divided into two basic costs, the manufacturing and the marketing or distribution.

Manufacturing and marketing costs vary according to the type of product. In some cases the marketing cost is even higher than the manufacturing cost. Marketing costs depend on the method of sales you are using. If you are selling on consignment through a shop, the shop may be taking as little as 20 or 25% of the retail price. If you sell to a store, the store might charge for your item twice what you were paid or even more.

If you are selling directly to customers, you may think you have no selling costs but you do have some. If you are participating in a show, you will not only have to pay any fees and travel expenses involved but you should also be paying yourself a salesperson's wage for going to the show, setting up, talking to customers, and sitting and waiting between sales.

Running a show of your own or selling through parties or personal visit takes time, so pay yourself for this time from the selling part of your price.

See Figure 2 for a sample of how you might figure your costs if you were making mobiles. Since materials are quite inexpensive, your costs might be even less than the 10¢ shown. If it takes you half an hour to make a mobile, and you price your labor as low as $1 per hour, you'll get a labor cost of 50¢ per mobile. If you can sell your mobiles for a higher price, you can increase the amount you receive for labor. On the other hand, you could earn more per hour by working more quickly.

Price for One Mobile	
Materials	.10
Labor ½ hr.	.50
@ $1.00/hr.	
Overhead	.03
Profit	.02
Total Manufacturing	.65
Selling Cost	.65
Retail Price	$1.30

Figure 2

Add a few cents for overhead and then, if you like, you can add a few cents profit. Profit is a sort of bonus for you in addition to your hourly wage. Consider it a protection against loss and a payment for your creative and management skills. If the project goes well, then you have the profit to invest in your next project.

Once you have your total manufacturing costs, then figure out the retail price of the item as shown in Figure 2. If you are selling wholesale the store will probably double your price so that the selling price would then be $1.30.

If you are running your own show or selling through flea markets or craft shows or using other sales methods, decide how much to add to the manufacturing cost to cover your selling costs. You could decide on one retail price and stay with it no matter how you are selling, or you might decide on a different retail price depending on your sales method. Probably a one-price policy is the easiest and best way.

What Will the Customer Pay?

One way to set your prices is to figure out all of the costs and add them up to see what your retail price should be.

The second system works in the other direction. First determine what your customer would be willing to pay, and then see if this price can cover the costs. To determine what the customer would pay, ask yourself what you might pay for one of your items without knowing how much work it took to make it or how much the materials cost. Ask people you know the same question.

See what your competitors are charging for a similar item. If your items are better because of workmanship, materials, or design, you should be able to get a higher price for them.

Remember that the customer usually does not know how much time or skill it took to make the product or the cost of the materials but only what he or she is willing to pay in order to own the item, to hang it on the wall, or to give it as a gift. Some people appreciate craftsmanship more than others, and if they are aware of how much work it takes to make an item, and how much skill is necessary, they may be willing to pay more.

At some shows and stores customers will pay higher prices than at others. In some areas you can charge more and still make sales. At a flea market, for example, the opposite is usually true—customers are looking for bargains and so if your prices are high you will probably not sell many items.

For some items customers may not be willing to pay what you would need to charge in order to cover your costs and labor. Can you find a way to reduce costs? Can you use less expensive materials? Can you cut down on the number of steps? Can you shorten the time necessary to make the item without lessening its quality? Perhaps the problem is that the customer can buy a similar item made by machine at a lower price. While your item is better, the customer may not be willing to pay a big difference in price.

When you find that you must charge too low a price in order to sell an item, don't make it. Or if you really enjoy making the item, continue to make a few as long as you have other items that you are selling at a good profit. The total of what you earn will be high enough to offset the lower price of the item you like to make, and you will enjoy the diversity.

Price Tags

Once you have decided how much to charge for a certain item, let people know. If you are selling through a store, the shop manager will probably take care of putting on price tags. If you are selling directly to customers at your own sale, or at a craft show or bazaar or through a crafts party or personal visit, let customers know the prices by attaching tags to each item or by putting a sign on a container of small items.

If the customer has to keep asking how much each one is, he or she will probably get discouraged and stop looking before buying anything. Customers like to see the items, know the price, and consider in private whether or not they want to buy.

Also, if your items are not marked with prices, you yourself may forget the price and quote a wrong one, especially if you are very busy. If you quote too high, you will probably miss a sale. If you quote too low, you will be cheating yourself.

Be sure that the price tags you attach do not damage the item. Make your own price tags or buy inexpensive ones at stationery supply shops. Use a small card attached with a little piece of string or a small sticky tag that comes off the item easily.

SIX

Advertising and Promotion

ONCE you get started selling, let people know about your business. You could make the most beautiful batik pillows ever seen, but if customers don't see them, you will never sell them.

There are many ways to tell people about your business and some of them you may already know about. Others you will discover. At first you may feel shy about trying to get publicity for your work. If you want to make sales, however, you need to build a reputation. The more frequently a customer hears or sees your name, the more chance there is that he or she will buy your work.

If you build a good reputation for yourself, people will think of you when they need to buy a gift. Therefore be as creative as you can in seeking opportunities and in creating them for yourself.

Your Image

Products have images (what do you think of when you hear "Cadillac" or "McDonald's"?). Manufacturers and retailers spend millions of dollars to create the desired image for their products or their stores. Press agents work to create certain images for their clients, usually politicians or movie stars. While you won't spend millions to create an image for your product and while you won't become a celebrity, you can create a positive image in your local area for both yourself and your work.

This chapter suggests ways of letting people know about your business. Use these methods whether you are working alone, with a partner, or with a whole group of people. Any group that wants to sell its work should have a good publicity chairperson who constantly looks for ways to tell customers about the group, its members, and the work they do.

The ways of telling people about your business can be divided into two groups, those that are free and those you must pay for. For example, in a newspaper you must pay for a classified ad, but in the same newspaper you might be able to get free publicity if you can get a reporter to write a feature story about you.

Opportunities for free publicity are everywhere but you must work to find them. Be creative in searching them out and persistent in your efforts to employ them. As far as paid advertising is concerned be selective as to how you invest your money so you get the most you can for it.

"Word-of-Mouth"

One of the best forms of publicity you can get is "word-of-mouth," one person telling another how good your work is. Because people usually believe what their friends tell them, they are likely to take the advice and buy your items.

"Word-of-mouth" publicity is a good reputation spreading. To earn this good reputation make a good product. If you use quality materials and your workmanship is good, you should be building a good reputation with each item you sell.

A good reputation also depends on whether you back up your work. If it is practical to do so, tell customers that if anything goes wrong with your product you will repair or replace it. If you put your name and address on the product or on its label, it is understood that you are taking responsibility for it and that if there is a problem you will correct it.

Give Your Business a Name

Before going out to get publicity for your business give it a name. While you can use a fanciful name like "The Purple Ostrich," it is a good idea to pick one that has something to do with your craft. Do not limit yourself by picking too narrow a name, for example, "The Batik Shirt Company." If you wanted to make batik pillows, for example, you would have to change it.

Do not use the words "Incorporated" or "Limited" in the name of your business. These are legal terms and if they are used in a business name they mean that the business is incorporated. Incorporation is a legal procedure handled by a lawyer. You are not ready for this and will not be incorporating your business unless it grows large.

Your Business Card

One of the cheapest forms of advertising is your business card. This small rectangular piece of heavy paper which you give to customers, shop managers, and others gives them the information they need to contact you. Make up the cards yourself by cutting small pieces of index cards and printing on them the necessary information. Later, if your business grows, a printer can make up cards for you quite inexpensively.

On your card put the name of the business as well as your own name and perhaps a title if you wish—are you the president of your company? Add your address and phone number. Decorate the card with a simple drawing, symbol, logo, or design you have made up to represent your company. It might show one of your products or have something to do with the name of your business. Use white cards or colored cards, or colored ink on a white card.

Use your business cards whenever you can. If you go to a shop to talk with the manager, give him or her your card. If you visit customers at home, leave your card so that they can call you when they might like to order.

If you run craft parties as described in Chapter 7, give customers your card or leave a small pile on the display so they can pick up one if they wish. At shows and sales, leave a small pile of cards on the table so that customers can pick them up.

Tell Your Own Story

Have you written your resume yet? A resume is a brief account of what you have done, usually including educational background, work experience, awards, club memberships and offices, hobbies and interests, and perhaps career plans. Resumes are usually composed by people looking for jobs, but craftspeople, too, often write up resumes.

You will find a resume helpful in different ways. Give a copy to shop managers when you ask for an appointment (see Chapter 9), so that they will already know who you are and what you have done before you come to talk. If you want to participate in a show, give a copy to the show director. Also give copies to your customers at shows and at your own sale.

You are an interesting person, so make your resume as interesting as possible. Do not be overly modest and leave out some of your accomplishments, but on the other hand do not overrate yourself. Tell about your school background, what grade you are in, what activities you are involved in, and what awards you have received if any. Tell how you happened to get started with your craft, how you decided to go into business, and how you have sold your items.

Make notes on what you wish to include. Number the points you want to make from the most important to the least and write them up in this order. Write simply and clearly. Ask someone to read what you've written and give suggestions. After your resume has been typed, make copies on a copy machine at first. Later you might want to have the resume printed up inexpensively.

Take Photographs

Start right away to take pictures of your work and of your displays at shows. They'll help you remember what you've made and some of the shows you've been in. Photos are also useful for publicity. If a newspaper reporter is writing an article about your work, he might appreciate a black-and-white photo to go with the story. If you want to enter a show, the director may ask for photos or slides of your work and of your display.

Use photos as a record of your work. If you make many different items, some of them as special orders, keep a photographic record of each type, and arrange the photos in an album. A customer who wants to give you a special order can often make a choice after looking at the photos.

If the items you make are large you cannot take many with you when you visit customers, sell at parties or at shows, or even when you go to stores. Take along your photo album in addition to the samples you can carry.

Fliers

Another inexpensive way to get publicity is to have fliers printed announcing your sale, explaining your craft parties, or listing items you make and their prices.

To be sure that the flier tells the story you want it to, think out your message carefully. Use words that will sell your work or bring customers to your event, ones that will set off a positive emotional reaction in the customer. Let people know what your products will do for them to make their lives more pleasant or to save them time and money. Cater to them as individuals and stress the personal nature of your service which is "designed just for you."

Before you write up copy for the flier, get together all necessary information. Be sure you haven't forgotten something important like your name or phone number or the date and time of the event—and be sure that your spelling and grammar are correct. Line drawings can make your flier more attractive. A sheet of paper 8½" x 11" is the most convenient size for reproduction purposes.

How you get the flier duplicated depends partly on the number of copies you will need. If you are working on a project with fellow students at school your teacher-advisor might have access to a ditto or mimeograph machine. If there is a duplicating machine in the school office, your group might get permission to use it. The group should of course pay for the paper used. If you do not have access to a duplicating machine and you need only a few copies, see if you can find a library, bank, or store that provides a copy machine for the use of the public; the charge is usually a small amount per copy.

Another alternative is to find a local print shop that does inexpensive offset printing. The larger the quantity you order, the lower the price per copy. For a little extra, the printer will use colored paper. If possible, arrange to do this. Colors evoke an emotional response. Bright colors like red, gold, and orange are eye-catching and can have dynamic impact; brown is low-key and respectable; blue and green are soothing and relaxing.

If you can give the printer an exact copy of the flier as you want it to look, he or she will be able to use a duplicating process. If you want the printer to set your words in type, however, or if you want to add a photo or a second color of ink, the price will be higher.

Classified Ads

The least expensive type of advertising in a newspaper is a classified ad. This is a good way for you to announce your own sale or craft party. These ads usually consist of about six lines of small print in a box. They are grouped or "classified" by subjects (Houses for Sale, Garage Sales, Help Wanted, etc.) and put in one section of the newspaper.

For classified ads you are usually charged by word. The larger the newspaper, the more copies that are sold on a daily basis, the higher will be the charge for classified ads.

Look in the classified section for instructions on placing an ad. The usual procedure is to call the newspaper and read your ad to someone in the advertising department, who then tells you what the ad will cost and sends you a bill.

Before calling, write out your ad. First read some of the ads in your newspaper to see how they are worded and choose your words carefully. Get the most information you can in the fewest number of words because each additional word costs money.

Feature Stories

Look at your local newspaper and see if it carries feature stories, often called human interest stories, about local people who are doing something different that other people in their area might like to read about.

Believe it or not, you are feature material for a newspaper once you get your business started. Newspapers often carry stories about young people vandalizing a home or school, creating disturbances, or terrorizing senior citizens. Editors are usually glad to hear about a young person who is doing something positive and creative— something that might interest other young readers as well as their parents.

Reporters, who write the feature articles, sometimes suggest ideas for stories to their bosses, the editors, so you can contact either a reporter or the newspaper editor. Don't be afraid to approach either one at your local paper.

If your business would make an interesting article, the editor or reporter will be glad you called.

If you are running a sale, try to have the article appear just before the sale. If you are working with a group, your publicity chairperson should send out announcements or press releases telling about your projects and inviting reporters and editors to call for more information.

To make the first contact you can either call or write a brief letter explaining a little about your business or the event you want to publicize. Write a press release or short article giving all of the facts. Write "Press Release" at the top and at the bottom write "For more information contact" and put your name and phone number.

If the newspaper is interested, a reporter will be assigned to the story or, if the newspaper is very small, the editor may tell you he or she would accept a longer article if you want to write it. If you have a good black-and-white photo, the newspaper may be glad to get it.

Approach only one newspaper at a time. Remember, the larger the newspaper, the less chance you have of getting an article into it. But don't be discouraged. If the largest newspaper refuses, go on to a smaller one.

You have the best chance with a small local newspaper, perhaps a weekly. Do you receive a free "shopper"—a newspaper consisting mainly of advertising from local stores? Often these papers have feature stories about people, places, and happenings in the area.

Once an article about your business has appeared in one newspaper, wait at least a few months before you approach another. Newspapers want to carry different features from those of their competitors.

Displays

A good way to get free publicity for your work is to put samples on display. Does your school have a display case, perhaps in the school library, where students' work can be shown? Town libraries usually have display cases and the librarian may be glad to have you put up an interesting display of your work, perhaps adding a few books from the library on your craft to add interest to the display.

Banks, museums, hotels, theaters, hospitals, and other public places have display space that you might be able to use. Wherever you see crafts on display, ask if you might be able to schedule a display of your own work. Also check with businesses, especially those like real estate and insurance offices that do not have merchandise to display.

When you have reserved a display area, look it over carefully and choose items which will fit well there. On each item put a small price tag. Put up a sign letting people know how to order the items displayed and possibly a copy of your resume.

Radio Publicity

Once your business really gets going and you have something to talk about, you might be interviewed on the radio. All over the country small radio stations are looking for interesting people to interview on talk shows. You are an interesting person. Probably not too many people your age in your area are in business for themselves. You are young, ambitious, and clever, and if you can answer questions and intelligently discuss your craft and your business, your local station may be interested in having you on a program.

Talking on the radio is not at all a frightening experience. If the program is live, that is, transmitted just as you are talking, you will probably be asked to come to the station a half hour early. That will allow you to meet and talk to the interviewer beforehand. He or she will give you some idea of the questions that might be asked. Of course one question usually leads to the next as in the normal flow of conversation.

You do not have to prepare for an informal interview, but think about the questions the interviewer might ask. How did you learn your craft? How long have you been doing it? How do you think up new items to sell? How do you sell your work?

When you are on the air you will sit in a small glassed-in room in front of a microphone. The interviewer will get signals from the technician running the program. A red light will probably light up when you go on the air. Before you know it the interviewer will be signaled that it is time for a commercial break. The red light will go off and the interviewer will relax and talk to you about what might be said on the next segment.

Setting up a radio interview is usually fairly easy to do at a small local station. It is of course much harder to get on large stations in the big cities.

It is a good idea to listen to the station and see if you can find a program on which you could be interviewed. Remember the name of the interviewer and write a brief letter to him or her. Explain that you would be happy to be interviewed and mention the subjects that could be discussed—your craft, how you got started, how you sell, local craft events, etc. If you have several friends who make and sell also, you could say that they would be available to be interviewed if the station is interested in a panel discussion. If you have written your resume as described earlier in this chapter, include a copy with your letter.

Write to only one station at a time. If you do not hear within three weeks either write again or call the station. If you still get no response try another station. Once you have been on one program wait a while before contacting another station. One station does not like to do an interview soon after its competition has interviewed the same person.

Be sure to tell the radio audience where they can buy your work, or let them know where to contact you to run a party (see page 65), if that is how you sell. If you can arrange to have the interview near the time of a sale you are running, or a show you are participating in, this will bring people to you.

SEVEN

Getting Started in Selling

ONCE you have developed a craft skill, made some samples, and decided on prices, you must find customers to buy your work. The more time and effort you give to your business the larger your total sales can be. There are several possible ways of selling.

Sales Methods

At first you may sell your work to friends, relatives, and neighbors when you happen to see them. You can call on people you know as a sort of door-to-door salesman, as described later in this chapter. Another possibility is to run craft sales parties. These are gatherings at private homes where you show and sell your work as described later in this chapter. At the first few parties you will probably know all the guests but later the guests may be strangers.

One way to sell to people you know is to set up a

57

display of items in your home and ask them to visit. You
could also advertise your sale and get strangers to come.
Running your own sale is described in detail in Chapter 8.

You may want to try selling through local stores as described in Chapter 9. Start going to flea markets, art and
craft shows, county fairs, and other similar events held
locally. If you think you would like to start selling by taking a booth at one of these events, then sign up and participate as described in Chapter 10.

You might eventually try all of the methods described
in this book or only one or two of them, depending on
your own personality and circumstances, as well as on
how much time you have available.

Use these same selling methods whether you are working alone or with a partner or group. Probably the most
popular way for a group to sell handcrafted items is to run
its own sale. But members of a group, acting individually
or in pairs, can also use other methods. The group could
sell through personal visit, or through parties, or to stores,
with one or two members bringing items made by all. The
group, as a unit, could enter shows, with a few members
going to each show to sell for the group.

Selling to People You Know

Before you start selling, you should know something
about the difference between selling to strangers and to
people you know. Your close friends and relatives will
want to buy something just because it is *you* doing the
selling. Many adults feel an obligation to buy when a
young person asks, whether it is Girl Scout cookies, a
chance on a raffle, or a box of chocolates—and often they
buy items whether or not they really want them. Be aware

of this and try not to take advantage of your relatives and neighbors. Don't ask the same people over and over to buy your work because some may feel obligated to buy every time.

Your aunt may gladly give you $5 for a decorative wall hanging you made to encourage you in your business, but she may put the hanging away in the attic. You really don't want to sell things that people will never use, things they buy only to be nice to you.

Your first customers will most likely be people you know. While selling to them is different from selling to strangers, take the opportunity to practice some of your sales techniques.

Always be ready to tell the customer the good points about your products, how they are unique and what benefits they offer, but let your items sell themselves as much as possible. Discuss them as something interesting you have been working on, not as something that the customer must buy. If you have to try to convince the customer that yours is a good product, then something is wrong.

Be ready to discuss your craft, how it is done, and the materials and equipment you use, but explain only if the customer seems interested. Be ready to answer questions and tell how to use the item, the various colors or styles available, etc., but don't put pressure on the customer to buy.

Selling to Strangers

While your relatives and friends may buy your items just because it is you who is selling them, strangers will not feel obligated to buy something unless they want it and are ready to pay the price. When you are talking to the first customer you don't know, you can feel confident if your products are good. You are not asking the stranger to do you a favor by buying your work; you are giving him or her the opportunity to buy a worthwhile, handcrafted item at a reasonable price.

If your manner and approach are polite and friendly, customers will be more apt to buy. You can encourage them with pleasant conversation, but don't make direct and embarrassing appeals for them to buy.

How you look and act is important. You are selling not only your work but also yourself as the one who made the items. If you are at a show, your customer knows of course that you made the items and will evaluate you, perhaps quickly and unthinkingly. Surface appearance counts in these situations. If in the customer's opinion you are neatly, cleanly, and appropriately dressed, you have a better chance of making a sale.

Your attitude is important too. If you are cheerful, confident, and positive in your approach, the customer will trust you and your work. If you act rude, impatient, insulting, or haughty, or seem distracted, the customer will not want to buy from you.

Don't be pushy. On the other hand, don't ignore the customer. Show interest in his or her needs and in your own products and act as though you are interested in selling them. Be thoughtful and courteous regardless of the amount of the sale. The customer who buys nothing today may give you a big order another day.

When you first meet shop managers and show directors, they may judge you by attitude and appearance, too, because they have only these by which to judge you. Once shop managers and customers get to know you better, they will see you as the person you are and no doubt will develop confidence in your workmanship and reliability.

If after speaking to you the customer walks away without buying an item, don't feel that he or she has rejected you as a person. Often people consider buying and then decide that they don't need the item or can't afford it. They may have liked you personally and liked your work but simply could not buy anything at the time.

In all of your dealings with customers try to be understanding and don't argue or insult. If someone bought one of your items and has a complaint, offer to replace the item, even if you feel that the complaint is not justified. It is important to keep the good will of your customers.

Look for Opportunities

Be alert to opportunities to sell your work. Do your parents run a store or a farm produce stand? Perhaps they will let you put up a small display of your work.

Can you locate any opportunities at school? How about selling your work at sporting events? Perhaps your school has football games or other events that draw a crowd. Sometimes sales booths and refreshment stands are set up at such events. What could you make to sell that would fit in with the event? How about pennants for the spectators to wave, or pins, hats, or corsages that show the school colors? Start a fad that sweeps the school. You might arrange with the team manager to sell your items and give a small percentage, perhaps 10% of your sales, toward team expenses.

Workshop-Display Area

One way to sell is through a small display right at the place where you work. Once you get busy making your items, you will need a special place to work. At first you may have to use the kitchen table, and put everything away at mealtimes, but of course this is not a good arrangement.

As soon as you really start selling, and you know you will continue your business, try to find and fix up a permanent place to work. You may have to do it right in your own bedroom. Or try to get permission to fix up part of the cellar, or use the spare room if your home has one. You will be able to work much more efficiently if you can get everything organized in the one place where you will work.

You need not only a workspace, perhaps a large table with a chair, but also storage space—a closet or some shelves. If there is still more room in your work area, you have a sales opportunity. Fix up a small display of items you have made. When visitors come to observe you as you work, they can see the display of items and perhaps buy some. If you are lucky enough to have lots of space available, you might even have a separate area divided from the workshop or even a separate room for display.

Selling Door-to-Door

Salesmen going from door to door selling their wares is an older tradition than the department store or the gift shop or the shopping mall. The traveling salesman sold to colonists long before stores were opened. Today some products are still sold door-to-door and perhaps you will find this a good way to sell your work.

Before you go out selling, prepare sample items to show your customers. You could either sell the items you bring with you or take orders, make them up, and deliver them later. If you are taking orders, bring at least one sample of each item you make. You could put a tag on each and record on the tag not only the price, but also what choices the customer has with regard to color and size.

Since you will be carrying the samples from one house to the next, look for a good way to pack them, so that they will not get wrinkled or dirty. You could use a small suitcase and arrange the items conveniently so that they are easy to get out and put back in place again.

In addition to having the samples, you could make a list of your items including prices of each and the choices of size, color, etc. Add your name and phone number so that your customer can contact you to give you an order. If you find the list useful, have it copied as described on page 51.

Another convenience is a simple order blank which you can make up yourself. Fill it in as you talk to your customer using carbon paper to make two copies, one for yourself and another for your customer.

Make a form something like the one shown in Figure 3. Leave a space at the top for the customer's name, address,

Figure 3

JOE'S WOODEN WONDERS

429 Hillside Ave.

Ringwood, New Hampshire 60621

SOLD TO: *Jane Forrest*
          97 North Bend Drive
          Ringwood

Number	Item	Unit Cost	Total Cost
2	*napkin holders* *#1 - red and white* *#2 - blue and yellow*	*1.50*	*3.00*
1	*clever clothes hang-up* *name "Bill"*	*3.50*	*3.50* *6.50*

Aug 7
Delivery Date

Jane Forrest
Customer's Signature

and phone number. Below this make four columns. The first should list how many of a certain item the customer is ordering. The second column should list the item itself and any special requests or personalization necessary. The third column should list the price per item and the last the total price for items of this type. Below leave a space for the total sale and the delivery date as well as a place for the customer to sign.

Selling Procedures

Whenever you go out selling, let your parents know where you are going. Visit people you or your parents know. The best time to catch people home is on weekends or at dinnertime in the evening.

When you come up to the house, knock at the door or ring the bell. Don't keep ringing but give the person a chance to answer before you ring a second time. Always be very courteous. Explain briefly that you are selling the items you have made. Ask the customer if he or she has a few minutes because you would like to show some of your work. If the person looks busy or hesitant, offer to come back at a more convenient time.

If the person is willing to look at what you have brought, take out your samples. Explain as you do that you are taking orders and that each item will be made especially for the customer as ordered.

As your customers look at your work, listen closely to their comments. One might say, "I would buy one of these except that . . ." Consider the problem and see if you could make changes so that this person and perhaps others would want to buy your work. Customers sometimes make very good suggestions for improving your products.

If the person finds nothing to buy, give him or her one of your business cards or a list of your products if available. You might say something like this, "Thank you very much for taking the time to look at my things. I would like to leave my card with you. If you want to order something at another time give me a call. My number is right on the card. Would it be all right if I came back again in six months or so?"

If the customer decides to order something from you, write down on your order pad what is wanted. Be sure to have the customer check what you have written and perhaps sign the order at the bottom. Tell the customer approximately when you will deliver the order, giving yourself plenty of time to make the items. If you find later that you are having trouble getting the items made up when you promised, don't hurry them and do a poor job. Instead call your customer and explain the problem. If the customer is agreeable, set a later delivery date. Never disappoint a customer by promising to deliver and then not doing it. Perhaps the customer was planning to have the item for a certain occasion. Try to please your customers with your work and by your reliability.

Build a following of customers from whom you can get repeat sales. Of course, you should not go back too often to the same customers and when you do, always try to have some new items to show.

A Party for Profit

One way to have fun and make money at the same time is to run a craft sales party, a method used to sell a variety of items including kitchenware, clothes, wall decor, and jewelry. The person sponsoring the party invites a group of friends to his or her home. After everyone has arrived, the salesperson makes a brief presentation, talking about the products and showing them. Anyone who wants to can order and then everyone has refreshments.

The sales party is a great way to sell, and more crafters are discovering it. You can do it alone or with a partner, inviting either young friends or a group of older people. You can run parties only occasionally or more often if you want to increase sales. You can sell only your own work or include items made by other crafters, keeping part of the price of these items as your fee.

Arranging a Party

The first party or two you hold will probably be in your own home with several close friends. If these go well, perhaps later several of these friends will be able to run parties in their own homes for you.

An arrangement to have a party is called a booking. If people learn you are running sales parties they may call to ask you for a booking.

The person who is running the party for you at his or her home is called the host or hostess. Give all the help the person needs. He or she should contact friends and ask them if they would like to come to the party and should tell them a little about your craft and the fact that you will be demonstrating how you do it. It does not matter how many people come; there might be only four or five or as many as twenty or more. While it is nice to have many people, don't judge a small party as a poor one. Sometimes small parties result in more sales than larger ones. In addition to inviting the people and providing the place, the host or hostess should also prepare some refreshments to serve after your presentation.

When commercial companies run parties the host or

hostess is usually given credit according to the total amount of the sales at the party. For example, he or she might get 10% of the total sales in credit and can then make a selection from the items on sale using that credit. You can make a similar arrangement or make a special host or hostess gift.

At the end of each party you might tell those attending that they can have similar parties in their own homes. The host or hostess is usually also given credit according to the number of future parties or bookings that are set up at the party. If you wish you could give the host or hostess merchandise credit—perhaps $1 for each booking.

At the Party

Before running a party, plan carefully what you will do. You could just display your items and let people look at them or you could make a short presentation, explaining and describing them, talking for just a few minutes but certainly not more than a half hour.

Your first party, probably in your home with just a few of your close friends, could be a sort of practice session for you. If you make a presentation, ask for advice on how you could improve it.

When you start going outside your home to give parties be sure that you arrive early, before the guests. Set up a small exhibit of your items marked with prices. Greet people as they arrive and make them feel at home. Encourage them to look at the display. If they are very busy talking, let them alone. The party should be a social event for them and your selling just part of it.

When everyone is there, begin your demonstration. First tell a little about the background of your craft if possible and about the materials and equipment you use. Bring samples of these so you can hold them up as you speak. If appropriate, pass around the samples so that those present can handle the materials and tools. If you do several crafts, talk briefly about each, but don't make your presentation too long.

Tell the group how you got started and how you do the craft. If you do original designs talk about them and show samples of your work as you speak. Hold up items from your display as you explain them and again let people pass them around if they wish.

Let the people ask questions and when you have answered them explain how they can buy the items you make. They can make their selections from the items on display or order special items in their choice of design or color. Perhaps your items are personalized in some way or perhaps they could be made to match the color scheme in a room. If you make bread-dough napkin rings, for example, you might have a blue and white set on display while a customer might want to order one in red and white.

Another way a customer could decide what to order is through drawings and photographs which you bring. If you have a notebook or photo album showing items you have made before, the customer can look at these and perhaps decide that he or she wants the same type of item or something similar. An album of photos showing your work is a good idea especially if you make larger items and cannot bring too many, or if you do not keep a sample of each design on hand.

Tell the customers how long you will need to make the items and set up a delivery date, being sure to give yourself enough time.

After the party, make up the orders and deliver them to the host or hostess, who might collect the money from the individual customers and have it ready for you when you make your delivery.

You will enjoy doing custom orders for people who have ordered through your parties. Making specific items for specific people you have met and can remember is a nice aspect of your work.

EIGHT

Running Your Own Sale

You can run your own sale of handcrafted items whether you are working alone or with a partner or with a whole group. The possibilities are endless and your sale can be any size you wish, lasting just a few hours or several days or even a week. You can have just a small display of items or a whole hall or field full.

Why Your Own Sale

There are many advantages to running your own sale. It can be lots of fun and it will give you a great sense of accomplishment especially if it is successful. You can display your items as you wish, taking the time to arrange them attractively. You will enjoy seeing the displays you have created and talking about your work to the people who come to see it. Be aware right away, however, that holding your own sale—in addition to being fun—is a lot of work, depending on how big a sale you are planning. Many different jobs must be done and if you are not willing to do all of them, you should not run a sale.

Running a sale is an investment in the future, if you decide to run it on an annual basis. Each year it can get larger and larger, so that the work you do to get customers to come to it this year, and the work you do to please them, will pay off when they come to your sale next year.

Ask neighbors, relatives, and friends to come to the sale and see your work. You have a better chance of selling to people you know than to strangers.

You can run a sale alone, but you probably will need some help, especially when the sale first opens. Perhaps a parent or some of your friends could help. If you are in business with a partner, running a sale together is a good way to sell your work. A sale is an especially good way for a group to sell handcrafted items. Each member can get involved in the project and since there are so many workers each one can help with the many jobs to be done.

Planning Your Sale

If you are running the show on your own, you will have a lot of planning and preparation to do. If you are working with a partner you can share the work. If a group is running the event, hold meetings so that everyone can help to plan for the event. As each aspect of the show is discussed, be sure that someone is writing down all the decisions that have been made and all of the assignments that have been given. If the group is very large, it might be a good idea to type these and give out copies.

One of your first decisions will be selecting a name for your sale. If you are running it alone, it might be simply "Bill's Sale" or "Barbara's Boutique." If your group is running it, get the group's name into the title, for example, "The Grant Street Crafters' Sale." If you plan to hold the show every year put the word "annual" in the title even the first year, for example, "The First Annual Plainfield Crafters' Sale."

One of the first decisions the group must make is who should be in charge. You need a show director who will oversee the whole event, make sure that everything that needs to be done is done, and make decisions when the group cannot meet to make them. If the director is a good leader and a person with initiative, common sense, enthusiasm, and willingness to work, then your show has a good chance to be a success. If you have a poor show director the event could easily flop. Therefore choosing the right person to be the director is vitally important to the success of your show.

The director must be supported by workers who are willing to take on jobs and do them. The main tasks to be done are publicity, display, and finance, so one person could be in charge of each of these. If you decide to have refreshments another person could be in charge of this area.

The whole group must decide if each person will have his or her own table and make individual sales, or if there will be one central register where all the money is taken (except perhaps for the refreshment stand which could be run independently).

It costs money to run a show. You may be able to keep your costs low, but if you have fliers printed, if you send out personal invitations, if you make posters, if you buy some display equipment, you will need to spend money. If the group has no treasury, each person might donate a small amount to pay expenses. If you are running the show by yourself, you alone will have to pay the expenses but, of course, your profit from the sale should more than cover them.

Whether you are running a big sale or a small one, you must prepare for it ahead of time. Make a list of everything you will need to do. Figure out what supplies you will need and plan to have them all at least two days before the show. Leave the last day free to take care of all the last minute details.

Also consider whether or not you will serve refreshments. If the event is held outside it is easier to serve refreshments because you don't have to worry about spills. You might decide to have free refreshments in order to tempt customers first to come and then to browse longer and perhaps buy. Or you might decide to have a refreshment stand as a money-making venture. Sell lemonade, iced tea, fruit juice, or cans of soda and perhaps cookies, too.

If someone in the group is a baker by craft, he or she could make cookies or cupcakes to sell at the show.

The Time

Probably the two most popular times for sales of hand-crafted items are the summer when the sale can be held outdoors and the fall months—especially November—when people are buying Christmas presents.

If you have been working on items all summer, you could have your sale right after Labor Day when the weather is still pleasant and everyone is home from vacation. Have it in the backyard in summer or early September, but be sure to schedule a rain date.

The weekend is the best time to have a sale because more people are at home and have time to come. If you are running the sale for several days, be sure that at least one of them is on the weekend. In deciding the time for the sale, take into consideration the hours you are free and the time when your customers might be available. If you are only going to have your sale for a few afternoon hours, from two to four is good—or noon to five, if possible. If the sale is held indoors, open in the evening from seven to nine.

Plan your sale at least a month in advance. You want to be sure that you have time to do everything, especially get publicity. Once you have run a successful sale, start planning another right away for the following year. It is never too early to start thinking about it.

The Place

Once you decide on a location for the sale, get permission to use it from your parents or through your adult sponsor.

If the weather is warm, have an outdoor sale. Customers enjoy coming to an open air market and if you are lucky enough to have a pleasant day and a good location, they may stay longer, browse more, and buy more.

Choose a place where there is plenty of room for what you plan. If yours is an indoor show, be sure to find a place large enough for your sale. If you try to put too many items or too many customers in a small space you will have problems.

If the sale is to be held in your home, use the family room or any other room that is easy to get to from the outside and is big enough for your sale. For a large sale use several rooms. If necessary put up signs so that customers know where to go and not to go. If you want them to go down to the basement put up a sign with an arrow pointing the way.

If your sale is to be held at school choose a room that will be large enough and ask permission to use it well in advance of the day of the sale.

Be sure to plan for your customers' needs. If they will

be coming by car, there should be a place for them to park. Be sure that lavatories are available.

To avoid complaints, be considerate of your neighbors. Long before the show, tell them what you are planning and invite them to come. If there is a neighbor who is likely to feel that your sale will create a disturbance, try to find a different location.

See Chapter 11 for information on zoning regulations that you should be aware of if your sale is in your home.

What Will You Sell?

One of the first decisions you must make about your show is what you will sell. Try to have items in a wide price range—inexpensive as well as more expensive—but many inexpensive ones because these are the items that will sell.

If lots of children will be coming to your sale, have inexpensive items that they can afford and would like. If you will have adults as well as children at your sale, you might have a special table of gifts for parents that children could afford. You might call it something like "The Under-12 Shoppers' World."

If you are planning the sale with a group, then you will of course sell items made by group members, probably a variety of kinds. If you are having the sale yourself, and if you make only one or just a few different items, you could ask friends and fellow crafters to sell their work through your sale. By selling the work of others in addition to your own, you can offer customers lots of choices.

If you are looking for crafters to participate, ask people at school and see if anyone does interesting craft work and would want to sell items through your sale. People you ask may tell you about still more crafters. Your art teacher may have some students to suggest. Look for variety, that is, for crafts different from the ones you do. Also look for quality. You may have to refuse a crafter if you feel his or her work is not good enough; be as kind as possible in your refusal. You want to maintain a standard and have satisfied customers. At craft shows you attend look for crafters who might like to participate. And of course all along the way invite people to come to your sale and ask them to pass the word along.

There are two different ways you could arrange to have your friends participate in your sale. One way is to ask each one to take a booth or table. Given a place to set up, each one would bring not only the items to sell but also a table or other display equipment and would sell his or her own items to customers. You would earn money not only by selling items in your own booth, but also by charging a small fee to those who have booths.

One problem with this way of running your sale is that you may have trouble finding crafters who will have enough to sell to set up their own booths. You will probably find many more who have just a small number of items which they would be willing for you to sell for them. The second way of running the sale, therefore, is to accept items from different crafters with the agreement that you will display them. If you sell them, pay the maker, but if the items do not sell, return them. With this arrangement all of the items would be together in the selling area, arranged as you find room for them. You would take care of all the sales.

If you are selling items for other people be sure that they understand the procedure and that you take a percentage of the selling price of each item. You might ask for from 10 to 25%. If you ask for 20% and if the customer paid $2 for an item, you would get 40¢ and the person who made it would get $1.60. This is quite reasonable and most crafters would be happy with this arrangement.

Every item at your sale must have a price tag on it. If

you want the crafters to put price tags on all of the items they bring, try to supply the tags. Explain that in addition to the price, they should write their initials or a code number you give them on each tag so that you will know whose item is being sold.

Crafters should make a list of the items they bring with a brief description of each type, the price of each, and how many of each type. Go over the list with the crafters when they deliver their work and ask any questions you might have about the items so that you will be ready to answer questions your customers might have. Keep the lists in a special place so you can easily consult them.

Explain that you will do your best to take care of the items they are bringing but that you cannot accept responsibility for them. Accept only inexpensive items, especially at your first sale. Later if your sale does get very big and your parents are helping you to run it, you could ask them to arrange special insurance for it. If you are holding a sale at your school, check with the principal. Most likely you will have to go through an official procedure so that the event is covered by the insurance that the school carries.

Planning Your Displays

In addition to getting your items ready to sell at the show, figure out how to display them. Customers will not expect professional displays like those in a retail store, but neat and attractive displays will help to sell your work.

In planning the display look over the location where the show will be held and check to see what is available right there. If the sale is held outdoors, use a fence, a clothesline, or even a swing set on which to hang items. Are there any trees or tree limbs which you could use for displays? Streamers and balloons add a festive touch to an outdoor sale. Figure out what decorations you need and be sure to buy them at least several days before the show.

If you are having the sale indoors see what furniture is already in the sales area. Clear out knick-knacks and other portable items, but use the big pieces of furniture that are left for display.

Put items in every possible space, even along door jambs and window sills. Don't waste the draperies—with permission, carefully pin lightweight items to them. If you have many small items use a large basket or any other big container to hold them. Put your sales table in front where you can welcome people as they come in and add up their purchases as they leave.

Of course you don't want to spend a lot of money on display materials, so be clever with what is available free or at low cost. Use makeshift shelves. Look for several wooden boards to use as shelves and separate them with bricks or coffee cans weighted with sand or even flower pots. You can use different items as shelf separators but use two of the same size item on any one shelf. Don't put delicate or especially heavy items on makeshift shelves.

If you participate in shows or if members of your group have done so, you might have some display materials available to use. Also use card tables, folding tables, and snack trays. If possible cover these with fabric to improve their appearance. If you can get some wooden boxes, these can be used as is or covered.

Getting Customers

You could have many beautifully made items displayed in a very attractive way, but if you don't get customers to come to see your display, you will not sell your work. Publicity is the most important job related to the show and if it

In setting up an indoor display, use all available space, even draperies.

Chests, tables, and other pieces of furniture hold displays of diversified items.

is not well done the show will probably flop. Reread Chapter 7 for ideas on publicity. Of course you will not use all of the methods described but will select those best suited to your personality or to your group.

Use as many publicity suggestions as you can because the more different methods you use, the larger the crowd you are likely to get. The larger the show you plan the more publicity you need for it, so get started as soon as you decide to have the show, many weeks or even months before it.

"Word of mouth," one person telling his friend about the show, is the most effective publicity you can get. People who know you are the most likely to come to your sale, and the people they tell about it are also likely to come.

If you are having your sale at school, you will be able to get publicity for it in other ways than if the sale were at home. Much will depend on who is to come. Will only students and teachers in your school come, or is the sale open to parents or even the general public?

Use all of the usual ways of announcing a school event including asking that it be added to the list of daily announcements. Put up signs all over the school wherever they are permitted. To draw attention to the sale, long before it takes place run a contest perhaps to name the event and offer a prize for the best name submitted.

If you are running the show alone or with your partner at one of your homes, start telling your friends, relatives, and neighbors about it right away. If a whole group is putting on the show get all the members involved. Tell everyone how important it is to constantly talk about the show. If each member does talk about it with great enthusiasm to his or her friends, neighbors, and relatives, they will be interested—excitement is contagious. They will want to come and will pass along the word to still more people.

Another way to pass along the information about your sale is to write it down. Make up fliers as described in Chapter 7. Be sure to have them ready very early so you can deliver them in the neighborhood or tack them up in the school.

When you talk to people about the show, give them a copy of the flier so they will have it to hang up at home. It will tell them the time and place and be a reminder to go. If anyone is willing to take more fliers, give him or her more to pass along to friends and neighbors.

If your local supermarkets or other shops have bulletin boards, hang fliers there. What about the craft supply shop? Do you know anyone who works in a factory or office which has a bulletin board for announcements? Staple copies of the flier on trees in the neighborhood but be sure to ask the homeowners' permission.

Another way to tell people about your show is to make up posters. Ask local store managers if you can put them in the store windows. If a manager feels the poster is too large, perhaps he will let you tape up one of your fliers instead. If you are working with a group, each person could put up a poster in his or her front yard or in a large front window if it could be seen from the street.

Extend personal invitations to special people whom you would like to attend your show including perhaps teachers from your school. Write personal letters and mail them or deliver them in person.

Another way of getting publicity is to have someone walk around the neighborhood wearing a sandwich sign, which has all of the necessary information neatly and attractively printed on two large pieces of cardboard. Attach them together at the top with straps that go over the person's shoulders. The sign wearer might ring a bell to get people's attention. Depending on the group, you might even organize a small parade that could go through the neighborhood carrying signs, letting everyone know about your show. For the parade, which should be lots of fun, use noisemakers or musical instruments to get people to come out to watch.

Another inexpensive way to get publicity for your show is through the newspaper. Look over the newspapers that are sold or delivered in your area. Some have a free listing of upcoming events. Usually the instructions are printed right with the calendar telling how to get your event included on the list. Call or write as instructed and be sure to do so early so that the newspaper will be able to use your announcement.

Try to get a feature story written about the sale as explained in Chapter 7. Also place an ad in the classified advertising section, running it for several days before the sale. Another source of publicity is the radio. Many local radio stations announce upcoming events. Listen to see if yours does. Usually the announcer, after reading the list, explains how to get your event listed. Send in the information early to be sure it gets announced.

On the day of the sale put up signs with large arrows showing people how to get there. If they must make several turns, tack signs to trees being sure that the arrows point the right way. Get permission from the owner, of course, before putting up a sign on his or her property.

Put up a large sign in the front yard of the house where the sale is taking place. People passing by may stop and come in.

Sale Day

On the day of the sale get started early so that you will be ready to open on time. If you have planned well everything should go fairly smoothly. Even if you were able to set up some of the displays the day before, you still may have lots of last minute details to tend to.

Decide beforehand whether or not you will allow "early birds." People often come before opening time in order to have the first chance to find the best items. Allowing them in early does not seem fair to those who have the courtesy to wait and come just at the time you said you would be open. If you refuse early birds they may come back, but they may not—so you must decide what to do about this.

At the sale, dress in a special way so that you will stand out as the person running the sale. A girl might wear a long skirt and a boy might wear a bright vest. If your group is running the sale, then the members might dress in a similar way so that customers will know who you are. You might also wear a small nametag. If you have wearable items on sale why not wear one? If customers admire the handcrafted belt you are wearing, explain that such belts are for sale.

Be sure there are enough people to help with the sale. The largest crowd often comes during the first hour, so plan for extra help at that time. Greet your customers in a friendly manner and thank them for coming whether or not they buy anything. Be ready to talk about the items on sale and answer customers' questions.

To add to the festive atmosphere of the show, members of the group might dress up as clowns and entertain the customers, especially the children. Or if several members are interested in puppetry, perhaps you could schedule puppet shows during the sale. This could be free or very inexpensive and would give children something to do while their parents browse.

If members of the group are talented musically, schedule performances. Also try to have members of the group give demonstrations of their crafts. Set up a schedule of special events and print a copy on a large blackboard or on pieces of poster board or even print up fliers. People may stay longer if they realize that in ten more minutes they can see a weaving demonstration or in twenty more minutes the children will be able to see a puppet show. And while they are waiting they will be looking at the things on sale and perhaps finding more to buy.

If you or someone you know has a camera, get some pictures of the event. Be sure to photograph your displays, if possible before the customers come. The photos will bring back memories of the show, and if you decide to have another event next year, they can be used for publicity purposes.

The Sales Desk

Set up a sales desk where customers can pay for their purchases on the way out. Have this well organized so that

*Nina Watrous, armed with pad and pocket calculator, writes up a
sale for a customer at a show held in her home.*

when customers are ready to pay, you have everything you
need right at your desk.

First get a box in which to keep the money and put in it
coins and some dollar bills. Few customers will be
giving you the exact change.

Get a sales pad at a stationery store, or use a pad of
plain white paper, to record the name and price of each
item the customer is buying. Sales pads are handy because
they are ruled with spaces to list the items and the prices.
They usually come with carbon paper so that when you
write up a sale, you can give the original copy to the customer and keep the carbon copy for your records.

In addition to a sales pad and change, you could also use a pocket calculator, a fairly inexpensive item well worth investing in, if you do not own one and cannot borrow one.

To wrap customers' purchases you might need tissue paper. Very necessary are some paper bags. Ask your mother, neighbors, and relatives to save them for you. You may be able to get two different sizes of brown bags sold by the package at the grocery store or buy some plastic bags in different sizes. Also if you sell larger items get some clean used cartons at a local store.

The Guest Book

When you have your first sale, the hardest job will be to get customers to come. The second year it will be much easier because you can invite those who came the first year. If they enjoyed your first sale, they will probably come again and bring friends if you ask them to.

In order to send out invitations the second year, you will need to know who came to your first sale. Get a guest book and ask customers to write their names and addresses. The book can be just a pad of lined paper, or some sheets of paper on a clipboard, or a guest book bought at a stationery store.

Encourage everyone who comes to the sale to sign the book. Put it in a place where they are sure to see it and put up a sign asking, "Did you sign the guest book?" As people are paying for their purchases, ask them if they signed the book.

The guest book will tell you how many people came to your sale. Next year use it to write personal invitations to your sale.

After the Sale

When the sale is over and the last customer has gone home, your work is not yet over. If other crafters sold through your sale or if your group ran the sale, the money must be counted and distributed to participants.

Each contributor must pack up what is left of his or her sale items and take them home. If you bought display materials just for the show and you plan to have another next year, pack them up and find a storage place for them. Return any display materials you borrowed. Be sure to leave the area exactly as you found it—or cleaner.

Another important job is taking down the signs. If you put up a set of arrows pointing the way, be sure these come down; otherwise, customers may arrive after the sale is over.

Finally be sure to let everyone who helped you know that you appreciate their contributions. Thank them in person or write brief thank you notes.

If possible, after the sale get together with those who participated and talk about what worked and what didn't work. Write down any good ideas you discover for making your next sale better.

NINE

Selling Through Stores

RATHER than sell your work directly to customers, you can sell it through stores. The first thing to be aware of about this method of selling is that the store will take up to half and sometimes even more of the retail selling price of each item. By selling through a store, however, you will be selling a group of items, rather than a single item, so your selling time will be much less than for other sales methods in which you sell directly to each individual customer.

Before dealing with a store, in addition to having good products you need to know how this method of sales works and what is expected of you.

Do Stores Want Your Work?

Perhaps you have wondered if stores work only with adults or if they would be willing to work with you. Many managers, especially of the smaller shops, are very willing to work with young people and are glad to give them a chance to make money and to learn about business.

Remember that the shop manager is in business to sell, and he or she cannot work with you if your items don't sell. If you have good products to offer, shop managers will be anxious to have them and thereby make money not only for you but for themselves. Shop managers need to know, too, that you are reliable and deliver on time and that your work is consistently good.

Finding the Right Store

As more and more people become aware of the value of handmade items, the number of customers who want to buy them increases and the number of stores selling them grows.

Many different types of stores sell handcrafted items and some of these are better markets for you than others. Finding the right one or ones is vital because it means the difference between no sales and an increasing number of them.

Certain shops are especially appropriate for you to work with when you first start selling. Others you will work with only after you have had lots of selling experience. If you know how the stores are different you will be better able to find the best ones for you.

If you live in or near a city, there may be many stores in which you could sell your work. If you live in a rural area the opportunities may be much more limited. Before trying to sell, go to as many local stores as you can and see what is on sale. Go to shops which carry handcrafted items and also those that don't now but might be interested in your work if it would fit in with the other items on sale. Once you know the possibilities, decide which to try first.

Your best bet for a first shop through which to sell your work is a non-profit shop like a women's exchange (this type of shop handles handcrafted items made by anyone, not just women), or a shop associated with a YWCA, women's club, or other service organization. Such groups run shops not to make a profit but to give crafters a market for their work. If the shop makes a small profit, it is often given to charity.

These shops are usually run by volunteers who do all they can to aid the new crafter because that is the person they are devoted to helping. They are usually quite interested in getting young people started in selling their work. A brief list of non-profit shops is at the back of this book. There are many others so see if you can find one in your area.

If there is no local non-profit shop, look for a small retail store, perhaps one specializing in handcrafted items. A small shop is a good place to begin because the larger the store, the larger the order you may be given. Later you will want bigger orders but at the beginning it is best to work on smaller ones. Also small shops are usually friendlier and more informal and are usually run by people who appreciate fine handwork and enjoy working with those who do it.

A small retail shop may be run by a craftsperson who is selling his or her own work. In order to have a variety of items, he or she might sell the work of other craftspeople. A craftsperson running a shop would understand your aims and problems because, like you, he or she is creating items to sell. He or she may be willing to give you advice on how to improve your products and where to find good supply sources.

Handmade miniatures are popular items in many craft shops. Here Lisa Tarman puts some tiny flowers on display. The same shop sells Janet Spring's dolls.

Some craft shops are run by a group of people rather than an individual. Sometimes they are craftspeople who have banded together to open their own shop and run it cooperatively so that they all have a good market for their work. If you find such a shop in your area, ask what you must do to become a member and sell through the shop.

Some stores sell handcrafted items along with manufactured items. Gift shops often have both types, plus cards and wrapping paper. The manager of such a shop will be interested in your work if he or she thinks the shop can make a profit selling it and may make suggestions for improvements.

Some shops sell only a small number of handmade items. Shoe stores might sell handmade leather belts. Clothing stores could sell handmade accessories. Plant shops might sell handmade plant hangers. You may have to convince the managers of such shops not only that your work is good but that it would fit in with the other merchandise being sold.

In addition to small shops there are also department stores that sell handcrafted items along with their other merchandise. These stores have buyers for each department who constantly meet with people who want to sell items to the store. A big department store is not usually a good place for you to start selling your work because if the buyer decides to order, he or she will probably order not three or five or even ten, but usually by the dozens. Also the store will require lots of paperwork from you and this must be done correctly if you are to get paid. When you start selling you are not ready to deal with a department store. First try to sell to small shops for a while.

While you may do very well selling your work to shops that regularly take handcrafted items, don't limit yourself to these. If you can think of a good gimmick, you might sell your work to businesses that would have never thought of handling handcrafted items.

Walk down the main street of your town looking at every shop, not just the likely ones but the unlikely ones, too. What about the car dealership—would this be a likely spot for your work? What about stuffed cars, or miniature cars? How can the car theme be carried out in your craft?

If you make inexpensive items, you might be able to sell them to a store or business, not to be resold but to be given away. To create good will, businesses often give gifts to clients, especially at Christmastime. For giveaways businesspeople are looking for something different and not too expensive, something that would remind customers of their business. What could you sell to a real estate office? How does the idea of a house fit into your craft?

Think about the name of the company, too. If a store is called "The Cricket Cage" can you make something with a cricket design on it? If you come up with something especially clever the manager might want you to make the item exclusively for his or her business. He or she might offer you regular orders if you make a particular item only for that store or business.

Selling Through Consignment

You can make two different sales arrangements with shops. The first, called consignment, means that the shop manager gives your work a chance to be bought—he or she has not bought it from you. You must leave your items in the shop and the manager will pay you only after the items are sold, if they are sold. If not you must take them back.

Choosing good shops in which to consign is vital because the risk is all yours. All the shop is risking is the small amount of display space given to your work. If the shop is all consignment, as are most non-profit shops, then your items should get fair treatment as far as display is concerned. In a shop using both methods there is a chance your items on consignment may get poor display space because the manager is more anxious to sell the items he or she has bought wholesale.

Since you still own your items on consignment, keep good records of what is in each shop so you can check on them. (See page 101.) Every time you deliver items to a shop in person get a signed receipt which lists all of the items you have brought. Every time you get a payment, note on your record which items have been sold. If possible, periodically visit the shop where your work is on consignment to be sure the items are still safe and on display. If they have not sold within a certain length of time, perhaps sixty days, you may want to pick them up.

While it has many disadvantages, consignment does have some advantages. It gives you as a beginner a chance. Perhaps the manager of the shop likes some of your items but is not sure that they will sell in his or her shop. He or she would not be willing to invest in them by buying them from you wholesale, but might be willing to give them a try on consignment.

Another advantage to consignment selling is that you get a greater percentage of the retail price of each item. If you sell your work wholesale, the manager of the shop will probably double that price for retail sale—that is, if you sell the item to the shop for $2 he or she will sell it to the customer for $4.

On the other hand, if you are selling on consignment, the shop should take less of the selling price. The typical consignment arrangement is that you get ⅔ of the price and the shop receives ⅓. If the customer pays $6 for the item, then the shop will take $2 for selling it and you will get $4 for supplying it. Some consignment stores charge a larger percentage, perhaps 40%. Others, especially non-profit shops, might charge as little as 20 or 25%.

Because of the disadvantages of consignment selling, many professional craftspeople refuse to use the method. However, you as a beginner will probably use it to get started. Try to get the shop manager to agree to wholesale terms once your products have proven to be good sellers.

While you are taking a risk leaving your items on consignment in a regular retail store, the danger is much less in a non-profit shop. There volunteers usually keep very careful records to be sure that you are properly paid for your items.

Wholesaling

Wholesaling is the sales method you use if you sell your items outright to the store, which then owns them until they are sold to a customer. With this method the shop pays you whether or not your items are sold. If your work doesn't sell, and the shop has to lower the retail price, you are not affected.

Wholesale selling has several advantages over consignment including the fact that usually the wholesale orders are for larger quantities than items taken on consignment.

Probably the biggest disadvantage to wholesale selling is that you receive a smaller percentage of the retail price. At first you might feel that the shop is taking too great a percentage of the selling price of your item. Consider that the store has many expenses to pay, however, including rent, utilities, insurance, salaries to sales clerks, and advertising. The profit the shop makes on the retail price of your items might be only about 5%.

Non-profit shops are usually run totally on consignment. Department stores buy on a wholesale basis. Small shops might be run either on consignment or through wholesale or a combination. With some shops you have a choice, but usually the shop manager will tell you whether he or she wants to buy your items wholesale or is willing to take them only on consignment. If your items sell well on consignment, the shop manager usually will want to buy them from you wholesale.

Selling to the Store

If you want to sell to a store, you must: (1) find the shop; (2) arrange to talk to the buyer, manager, or acceptance committee; (3) convince this person or group to accept your work; (4) take the order; (5) deliver or ship the items; (6) be sure that you receive payment.

While later you may work with distant shops, mailing your items to them, at first you will want to sell to local stores. Visit shops and look around at the type of items for sale. Would your work fit in?

If you want to sell through a number of different shops keep good records of all you have visited. In a notebook or on index cards list the name, address, phone number, and manager's name if known. Write down your impressions and comments on the shop. If someone you know recommends a shop write down the complete information so that you can visit it. Ask crafters you know about shops which they think might be interested in your work. Look in the Yellow Pages of your phone book under "Gift Shops."

Once you have decided on which shop to try first, either phone the manager or call on him or her in the shop and see if you can arrange to come and show samples of your work. Then prepare samples to bring, arrange them neatly in a suitcase or bag, and know what prices you are asking. If the manager or buyer wants to buy wholesale, prices could be marked on a tag on each sample. For small items figure out a per dozen price. If the manager will take your work only on consignment, tell him or her that the retail prices are double your wholesale prices.

The first time you try to sell your work to a shop you may feel shy and nervous. Try to relax. This sale is not as important as it may seem right now. Remember you are not asking the shop manager to do you a favor but are giving him or her a chance to make money by selling your work to the shop's customers. You both should benefit by the arrangement.

If you are going to a non-profit shop, expect a pleasant experience. The volunteers who talk to you will probably be eager to help you and will be happy to take your work if they think they can sell it.

While you may hope to sell to every shop you go to, this is certainly impossible. Not even the best craftsperson can sell to everyone. Expect that some shops will reject your work. There are many reasons a shop manager may refuse your work in addition to the fact that he or she personally may not like it. Even a manager who does like your items may be concerned that not enough of the shop's customers would like them. Or the manager may not be buying new stock because he or she has too many items on hand. Or you may have come at the wrong time of the year. Remember, shops buy seasonal items months in advance. They are not looking for Christmas items in November, but much earlier during July, August, and September.

If you want to make a sale you must make a good impression on the shop manager or buyer. He or she may at first be very surprised to see how young you are. Don't let this reaction upset you but go ahead with the business at hand. At first the manager may be doubtful about working with you, but he or she will gain trust in you if you come prepared and act as if you know what you are doing.

When speaking to the manager be businesslike in your approach and in your conversation. Don't expect special treatment just because you are young. Don't use slang or poor grammar or giggle but don't try to sound like a walking dictionary either.

Greet the manager or buyer by name and introduce yourself. Be friendly and straightforward. Ask where you can show your samples. Take them out carefully and unwrap them if necessary. Handle the items carefully so that the buyer will see that you have respect for your work.

Before you can sell to the manager you must first convince him or her that your items will fit into the shop well. If you have looked around the shop beforehand, you will be able to talk about how they would fit in. The manager will be looking for a profitable addition to the shop's inventory, items that are different from what is on sale already, and items that are priced right.

As you are convincing the manager on all of these points and commenting on how worthwhile your products are, you are engaging in sales talk. You could practice a little beforehand, but you should sound natural and relaxed. You will not say the same thing every time, of course, but will use your judgment as to how much to say and how to say it, taking cues from what the manager or buyer is saying to you. The more practice you have, the easier the job will be.

If it seems that the manager is not going to buy, don't get upset. Keep your good humor and restrain your disappointment. Thank him or her for looking at your items and say that you would like to come again some time in the future when you have new items to show. While your first refusal will be a difficult one to take, don't forget there are other shops and perhaps the next one will order from you.

If on the other hand the manager is ready to give you an order, be ready to accept it. If the prices are not on tags attached to your items, be sure you know what they are.

Be definite in giving the prices and don't make excuses or try to explain your price. If you don't have an inventory of items all made up and ready to sell, know how long it will take for you to make the items. When the manager asks how soon you will deliver, be able to give a realistic date.

Once you have discussed what the manager is ordering and when it is to be delivered, the next step is to get the order in writing. A larger store may give you a purchase order with a number on it and this number must be on your bill. If the store does not give you a purchase order, have order forms of your own which might look very much like the order blanks you used for selling door-to-door as on page 63. Use two copies with a piece of carbon paper between them.

Be sure to get down all of the necessary details including the delivery date, the quantity and a description of the items, the choice of color if you are offering a choice, and the total price of the order. Also ask when the shop will be paying (usually within thirty days of delivery) and write down that information. Once the order is written, sign it and ask the manager to do the same. Give him or her a copy to keep.

The first sale you make to a store is of course the hardest one. Once the store manager has had a good experience with your products and with ordering from you, your selling job will be much easier. The next time you go to the store, the manager may be very glad to see you. And do go back to try to make more sales; even if they do want more of your items, stores will seldom call and ask you to come.

To keep the store manager satisfied and to get good reorders, do everything you can to maintain a good relationship. When you deliver an order, be sure that every item is as well made as the sample you showed to the manager when you took the order.

Delivery dates are important. If you have promised

items by a specific date, have them there then. If there is to be a slight delay, call the manager and discuss the problem.

Do not overestimate what you can do. The store will give you a delivery date, usually about two weeks from the time you take the order, and if you do not deliver the items by the specified date, the store can refuse them when they do arrive. And if you are late you will lose the manager's confidence in you.

When you are accepting the order, if you are not sure you can deliver when the manager wants the items, discuss the problem right away and perhaps you can find a solution. The manager may let you make two deliveries, a partial one on the date he or she wants the items and the second a short time later.

Also maintain your prices. Don't sell the same item to two different shops at different prices. If you do, and if the manager finds out that you are selling to another shop for less, he or she may not order from you again. If you are selling your items at a show near the store, charge the same prices as the shop charges.

Getting your work accepted in a non-profit shop or a cooperatively run store is usually a somewhat different process than approaching a regular retail shop. Rather than a manager or buyer choosing merchandise, it is usually a committee that decides whether or not to take your work. At some shops you must leave sample items, but at others you can talk to the people making the decision.

Some non-profit shops have certain set hours when those who want to sell their handcrafted items can come and talk with the person or committee in charge of accepting merchandise. This meeting could be very helpful to you. Looking at samples of your work, committee members will decide if they are willing to give it a chance in the shop. They can tell you if they think it will sell and if they think the prices you set are good. Any suggestions they may have for improvements could help you. Cooperatively run stores usually also have an acceptance committee to whom you must show your work before you are accepted as a member.

Keeping Good Records

Once you deliver or mail your items to shops, you are not finished. Now you must be sure that you get paid for the items. It is vitally important to the success of your business to keep good records of your sales to stores, whether you are selling on consignment or on a wholesale basis. Keep a record so that you know what you sold to each store and when, and if and when you got paid for the items. When you are trying to decide if and when to go back to a store for reorders, your records can help you.

If you are selling through consignment you should receive periodic reports from the stores that have your work. Each shop has its own reporting method. The shop will probably give you a copy of its consignment rules and this will tell you when to expect a report. If the manager does not have a definite set of consignment rules and a regular system of reporting to consignors, perhaps the shop is not run very efficiently and this might indicate that it is a poor one to work with.

Every month or two you should get a report listing the items sold since the last report, along with a check for the amount of the sales minus the percentage charged by the shop. Keep good records so that you will know when the reports are due from each shop where you have your work on consignment. If a report is overdue by a week or two, call the shop. There is reason to be concerned because stores do close and if a shop that has your items on consignment closes, you may never be able to get either your items or the money due you.

If you get a report and you find that your items are not selling well, visit the shop again. Bring different items if possible to replace things which have been in the shop for over sixty days and have not sold. If certain items have been selling well, bring more; the shop manager will probably want them. In fact, he or she may want to start buying them from you wholesale in order to make a larger profit on each item.

If you sell wholesale, you will usually not get paid on delivery or when you ship your items unless you demand payment on delivery. Stores usually are not willing to pay immediately but expect to billed and then given thirty days to pay.

Make a list of all of the items you are going to deliver to the store and have the person who orders them sign a copy of the list. Later when you ship items, enclose a copy of the list inside the package itself or in an envelope attached to the outside. This list is called a "packing slip" and if the manager finds any item on the list missing from the package he or she must let you know right away.

You can send a bill to the store the day you ship or deliver the items. Buy "invoice" forms at a stationery store. These forms have a space for your name and address as well as the name and address of the shop, the order number, the items bought, their prices, and the total sale. If you had to ship the items, the shop usually pays postage, so add this amount to the bill.

The form may also have several other spaces to be filled in. Fill in the one marked "shipped via" with "Parcel Post" or "U.P.S." (United Parcel Service), whichever you used. The abbreviation "F.O.B." which may appear on the form is short for "Free on Board" or "Freight on Board." If the shop is paying the postage, you list your town in that space. If you are paying, you write the name of the town where the shop is.

In addition the form may have a space marked "terms." The most common terms for crafters wholesaling to a shop are "Net 30 days" which means the store should pay the full bill within thirty days. Some craftspeople use the terms "2/10/30" or "2% 10 days, net 30 days" which means the shop can take 2% off the bill if it is paid in ten days or must pay in full in thirty days.

Keep your copies of the invoices in one place and be sure to mark them paid when the payment is received. If you do not receive payment within thirty days send a re-minder, another copy of the invoice marked "Past Due." Most shops will cooperate and pay their bills. You should not give a shop any more of your work, of course, if it has not paid the last bill. If in some instances you have trouble getting a shop to pay, you can threaten and then actually take the shop manager to small claims court as described on page 128.

TEN

Participating in
Flea Markets, Fairs,
Bazaars, and Craft Shows

RATHER than running your own sale, you may prefer to participate in a sale run by someone else. That person should provide the place, the advertising, and the customers. In exchange you will pay a fee to sell your work at that show.

All kinds of shows and sales are run varying in size from a few tables set up in a school hall to hundreds of booths at a regional craft show or a state fair. Shows include bazaars, flea markets, school fairs, art and craft shows, cultural exhibits and sales, county and state fairs, etc. While these events are different from each other, they all serve the same purpose for you—they bring customers in contact with your work.

Shows are a good way for you to sell because you can really test your products through direct contact with customers. Shows give you a chance to meet and talk to other crafters and even full-time professional craftspeople. This conversation can be very valuable; you can learn much from others who might be having the same problems as you.

Shows can be lots of fun. If you go with a parent or

friend, you can take turns walking around and enjoying the show. If you go to a number of shows you will start to make friends among the crafters and you will enjoy seeing one another again.

Before participating in shows, go to as many as you can as a customer. Carefully observe what is being sold and how crafters are displaying their work. See what they have done, not to copy them, but to get inspiration for items to make and the type of display to prepare when you are ready to use this sales method yourself.

Most shows are run on the booth method—that is, you pay a fee to rent a space. Within that space you can set up whatever you want, usually a table with your items neatly arranged on it or perhaps a standing board with items hung on it.

Janet Albury hangs a stained glass ornament on a display panel at the annual Outdoor Festival of Art in Plainfield, New Jersey.

If you participate in a show you will have lots of work to do beforehand. You must prepare an attractive display and make up enough items to sell. You must usually be at the sale the whole time the show is open plus time before and after. If you have a partner you can take turns being at the booth, except when things are busy or when one is demonstrating.

While most shows are run by the booth method, a small number are run on a consignment basis. You do not have to attend this kind of show. Before it opens, you deliver your items, each marked with a price, together with a list of the items brought. Those running the show will put your items on display and sell them if possible. When you come back to pick up the unsold items, you should be paid for the sold items minus the percentage which the show directors charge. The procedure is easy and similar to selling on consignment through a store—in this case, a temporary one.

Types of Shows

All over the country shows and sales are held year round in downtown shopping centers, malls, schools and colleges, church and synagogue halls, and open fields.

One way these shows differ is in what is for sale. At flea markets almost anything can be sold including food, antiques, old books, used furniture, and handcrafted items. Sometimes you can do well selling your work at flea markets, but only if your items are low in price. Many people come to flea markets looking only for bargains and sale merchandise and they may pass you right by if you are selling more expensive handmade items.

In some areas flea markets are held every weekend all summer long. If there is such a weekly market in your area, go to it as a customer first and see how many craftspeople are selling there. Talk to them if possible and see how they are doing. See if customers stop to look at and buy handmade things. If they do, this might be a good place to try out your merchandise. The fee is usually small.

Another type of sale in which you might be able to participate is a bazaar. Held by church and synagogue groups, women's clubs, senior citizens organizations, and many other groups, these bazaars usually have booths featuring many different items. Since crafts have become so popular some bazaar committees have started to allow craftspeople to participate. You must pay a small fee to set up your table and sell. The fee goes to the worthy cause for which the bazaar is being run.

Does your own school or any other local school run a fair? These are similar to bazaars except perhaps that there are more games for children to play and more things that children can buy. Find out if you could have a table at your school fair.

Other possibilities are county and state fairs which, like flea markets, have many different types of items on sale. Find out if many crafters sell at the fair nearest you and if their booths are grouped together. Some fairs are good for selling handcrafted items, others are not.

Though at most flea markets, school fairs, bazaars, and county fairs crafts are only a small part of the show, some shows feature crafts almost entirely. Often it costs more to be in such a show, but the opportunity is usually worth the fee. Most customers there are interested in crafts and not just looking for bargains. At such shows you will find professional craftspeople who usually do not participate in flea markets and similar events.

Another way shows differ is in the people who are running them. Art and craft shows are often managed by professional show directors who earn their living in this way. Others are run by amateurs, usually non-profit groups like women's clubs and religious organizations making money for their treasuries or for a good cause. Sometimes they are run by an art and craft group or by the Chamber of Commerce.

Some of these shows, especially those managed by art and craft associations, are judged and prizes are given for the best exhibit and/or for the best items on display in various categories. See if there is a junior division for awards. If so, this would be an especially good show for you to enter.

Many shows are open—that is, anyone can enter who applies in time, providing there are still booths available. Some open shows limit the number of people doing the same craft, accepting entries only until the quota in a specific craft is filled.

Some shows are juried—that is, only the craftspeople who are chosen to participate may do so. These are usually the best shows—those that everyone wants to get into. The judges usually choose entrants on the basis of color slides submitted by each craftsperson.

The first show you enter will probably be open, rather than juried. Most open shows are happy to have young people participate. Juried ones also accept young people but only if their work measures up to the standards set for the show. A juried show is then a goal toward which you might work.

Don't limit yourself to shows and events at which craftspeople are expected to be. Look for opportunities. If you see that an event is scheduled and feel that it might be an opportunity, try to discover who is running the event and find out if you can be part of it.

Finding Out About Shows

If you want to participate in a show or other event you must find out about it weeks in advance so that you can apply and get your items and display ready for the show. Some local newspapers tell about upcoming events and give information on whom to contact if you want to participate. You may see a sign for a show in a store window weeks before the date; if so, try to get enough information so that you can contact the person running the show.

Some shows are held every year at the same time. If you attend one this year as a customer, find out who is running it and if possible give the director your name so you will be notified in time to participate next year. Keep a folder of information on all of the shows you go to and all you see written about in the newspapers. This folder will be a valuable source of information if you decide to participate in many shows.

Another good source of information is other crafters. If you start talking to crafters at one show, you will find that they often tell you about other shows coming up.

Also if you join a craft guild or a local art and craft association, you probably will hear about upcoming shows in your area. Your local Chamber of Commerce or your State Arts Council might also help.

Some craft magazines like *Creative Crafts* and *Decorating and Craft Ideas* give lists of shows. If you become very interested in participating in shows, subscribe to one of the magazines or newsletters that specializes in telling craftspeople about shows. A list of these magazines appears in the Additional Information section at the back of this book.

Picking a Good Show

At a single show you might sell nothing at all or you might sell out your entire stock. Usually the result is somewhere between these extremes. Some shows are excellent, others are OK but some are very poor. Since you want to avoid the poor ones and participate if possible in the excellent ones, picking the shows to attend is very important. Become conscious of the differences among shows and aware of which ones are best for you.

It is impossible to know beforehand how well you will do at a specific show, but with experience you will be able to judge which should be good. If you pick a poor show, don't worry. The luck factor is definitely involved and you cannot be lucky every time. Even experienced craftspeople make mistakes and go to a poor show sometimes.

The time of year when the show is held is a major factor in its success. The weather of course is another factor. Shows are held all year long but probably those with the highest sales are held in the months before Christmas when people are looking for special handcrafted gifts. Summer shows are also popular because they can be held outdoors. Gift-giving occasions like Mother's Day, Father's Day, weddings, and graduations help spring shows succeed. Even Easter can generate the buying of small presents for children. Shows held early in the year are usually not as successful as those held in the fall.

Another difference among shows is that some are held only once but others are held every year. An annual event may be very successful because customers look forward to it and come every year.

If you are deciding whether or not to participate in a specific show, find out as much as you can about it. Did you attend it last year? Were there many customers and were they buying? If you did not go to the show, did one of your friends, or do you know any crafter who might have been there? Does the customer have to pay a fee to get into the show and if so, will that keep people away?

If you can talk to the show director, ask how many people came to the show last year. Consider where it is being held and how much publicity the director is getting for the show. Critical to the success of a show is good publicity especially if it is held in a church hall, or someplace people would not normally be passing.

Once you've decided that you would like to enter a specific show, write to the director. Explain what craft you do and what type of items you make. Tell why yours are different and interesting. If you have participated in shows before, say so and mention some of the better shows. If you belong to any clubs or associations mention these and include a copy of your resume and any newspaper publicity you might have received. If time is short you may have to call instead of writing. You should receive an application to fill out and return with payment for your booth.

What Does It Cost?

Shows can cost from nothing at all to hundreds of dollars. Some groups run craft shows to teach people about crafts and they may not charge you anything to participate, especially if you are willing to work on your craft and explain to customers what you do.

Directors of shows that do charge fees use two different methods, percentage and booth fee. Those who require a percentage of your total sales may also charge a small registration fee which you must pay before the show. After the show you must add up your sales and give 10% or whatever percentage is required.

Most shows charge a "booth fee" or "table fee," rather than a percentage of sales. The fee is the same for all crafters no matter how much they sell. Shows held indoors usually charge a higher table fee than those held outdoors. Shows run by non-profit groups tend to charge less than those run by professional show directors. The fee for a craft show might be double that for a flea market.

Note that the table fee is not the only cost you will
have if you are going to participate in a show. Remember
you must get to the show and home again. If a parent or
another adult drives you, the cost of the gas used is part of
your expenses. If the show is far away, you may have to
stay overnight and unless you camp or stay with a friend,
expenses will be high. Be sure to count travel expenses
including meals eaten out when you consider the cost of a
show.

Preparing Your Booth

At most shows you will have your own booth, usually a
space about ten feet long and eight to ten feet deep. In
that space you can set up a table or a display board or
whatever you like.

Having an interesting and neat booth is important; it
can mean the difference between a sale and no sale. The
general overall appearance of the booth will bring customers in to take a closer look. If from a distance your
booth looks cluttered, messy, and uninteresting, customers may not come any closer to see what you are selling.

Most craftspeople use a table, and if they often go to
shows they usually buy a lightweight eight-foot folding
table that is easy to put up and take down. As craft shows
often last all day you will need a comfortable chair. A lightweight folding lawn chair is good. To cover the table use a
long piece of solid color fabric. At first you might use a
sheet, but if you are going to many shows buy a piece of
quality material in a fabric store in a color that provides a
good background for your items. Keep the fabric as clean
and unwrinkled as possible. It should not only cover the
top of the table but drape down almost to the floor in the

front and at the sides. If the fabric brushes the floor on all three sides, you will be able to store boxes and supplies under the table.

You may also need boxes or baskets or whatever to put your items in or on. Exactly what you need will depend on what you are selling. You might also like to make up a sign for your display, perhaps using your craft technique. Put on it your name and/or the name of your business.

When you are planning your display think about adapting it to different situations both indoors and out. Remember that you have to bring it to the place where the show is being held and set it up. Be sure that everything you plan to take fits into your parents' car or the car of the person who has agreed to take you to the show.

Also try to plan a display that goes together fairly quickly and easily. Otherwise you will be wasting a lot of time setting up your exhibit and taking it apart.

Look for the best way to show your items. If you plan to go to quite a few shows, work at devising some interesting display equipment. Use household items like small bookcases or a jewelry box. Use ordinary materials in interesting ways.

When you set up at the show, keep some of your stock in boxes under your table. Display only one or several of each type of item. Keep the overall appearance of the display in mind. Too many items make it look cluttered and confusing. If a customer expresses interest in an item you can explain that you have it in other colors and bring out more items if the customer wishes to look further.

What to Bring to the Show

It is a good idea to make a list of everything you want to take to a show. You have four types of things to bring: (1)

Pottery is well suited to outdoor display.

items to sell; (2) display equipment; (3) sales equipment; and (4) personal items. Just before you leave, check the list to be sure that you have everything.

First, get quite a few items made and ready to sell. No one can tell you how much you will sell, but try to have a variety of different items, at least a few of each thing you make. If you make only one type of item, could you make it in several different colors so that your customers could choose their favorite?

Make a list of all of the items you are taking to the show. Each item should have a price tag on it unless it is in a box or basket with a large price sign.

Bring along a chair and the display materials and equipment needed to set up your booth. Bring extra paper and felt tip pens for making small signs. Bring tape, pins, and other such items you might need.

You will need a money box; empty cigar boxes are often used. Start out with some change and dollar bills in the box. Bring enough change so that you will not lose a sale or have to run around from booth to booth asking other craftspeople for change.

Bring paper and pen to record your sales. Use a sales pad and write up a slip to give to each customer, keeping a carbon copy for yourself. If you do not have a sales pad at your first few shows, use ordinary paper to list and add up the prices of the items each customer has bought. A pocket calculator is helpful. On your list of the items you brought to the show put a mark beside the name of the item when you sell one.

If the sale will last all day, consider your personal comfort. You will need to eat lunch. Pack a sandwich and bring along some snacks to munch on when you get hungry. Sometimes food is available at shows but often it is of poor quality and over-priced.

Keep in mind where the show will be held. If it is going to be outside you might need suntan lotion and a hat or even an umbrella to keep the sun off your head. If rain is predicted bring a piece of plastic to cover your items quickly if a downpour comes before you can get them packed away.

If your craft can be done while sitting at a show, bring along some work to do. Sometimes only part of the process can be done there but if you have this work along, you will not waste the time between customers.

What to Wear

Some show directors do not want craftspeople to dress too casually. Bearing this in mind, dress comfortably according to the weather forecast. Take an extra sweater if you think it might get cooler. Once you are at the show you will be stuck in your assigned place quite a while and you will be much more comfortable if you are dressed appropriately.

You may want to develop a special costume to wear at craft shows in order to attract people to your booth. If so, try to develop a costume that would fit in well with your craft or perhaps would suggest the name of your business. At some shows you will be required to be in costume. If the show has a specific theme, for example "Colonial America," you might be asked to dress in clothes reminiscent of that era.

Following the Rules

Some show directors supply a printed list of rules with the application blank. Read them carefully before the show and be sure that your booth complies with them. If you want to be in the show again next year, this is important. Even if a formal list of rules is not in force, the show director will expect you to follow customary procedures without being told what to do.

One important rule is that you arrive on time. The director may ask you to come an hour before the show is scheduled to open in order to set up. Of course, the first time it will take you longer to do this, but with practice you will be faster. Be sure to allow enough time so that you are completely set up and ready to sell when the show opens. Allow a few more minutes than you actually need because something may go wrong or you may find that something is missing.

You are usually asked to cover your table with a piece of clean, ironed fabric, draped to the floor on three sides of the table. You are expected to keep your items neatly displayed at all times and to be at your booth during the hours the show is open. If you must leave it briefly, your neighbor crafter or your friend or parent should be watching it.

Another unwritten rule at any show is that you should be considerate of other crafters. Cooperation is important. At many shows craftspeople cooperate beautifully, doing each other many small favors.

Craft show directors may have rules about what may be sold at their shows. For example, some require that the crafter who is selling the item must be the one who made it or that nothing made from commercial molds or kits be sold at the shows. Note that at flea markets, bazaars, and similar events these rules are usually not in effect.

Can You Demonstrate Your Craft?

At many shows you will be encouraged to demonstrate your craft. Some craft show directors are particularly anxious to have you do so because it adds to the atmosphere of the show and educates the public about crafts.

If you have a craft which you can do as you sit behind your table of wares, this is a good way to get people interested in your work. Some crafts cannot be done at a show, but there might be a portion of the process you can do at the show.

As you work people may gather at your booth. In fact, you may draw a crowd, especially if it is interesting to watch your craft being done. After they have watched and asked questions, people will probably want to buy.

Since while you are demonstrating you will have to pay attention to your work, have someone else at the booth to make sales and to keep an eye on the customers. Shoplifting can be a problem.

You might want to demonstrate, too, how your items work. If you sell puppets or marionettes, for example, have a puppet on your hand as you talk to customers. If you walk your marionettes around the area in front of your booth, you are sure to have customers watching.

Dealing with Customers

If you want to make sales treat prospective customers with courtesy and consideration. They may ask the same questions over and over. If this gets to be a nuisance, why not answer these questions on the label attached to your product or make up a little explanatory sign for your table? Every time you are asked certain questions, you can then point to the sign.

Greet customers with a smile and encourage them to browse. Be friendly but not overly so. If a customer looks toward you, smile and make a general comment on the weather, the show, or whatever seems appropriate. While it is fine to talk to your friends or fellow crafters when you are not busy, when customers arrive pay attention to their needs or you may lose sales.

Most of the customers you will meet at shows will be kind and considerate so don't be upset if you encounter one with poor manners. If two people are looking at your work, for instance, one might very loudly say something insulting about it to the other. Such incidents are rare, but be prepared for them. Ignore such people and don't argue with them. Don't let such comments worry you. Although this person did not like your work, others have liked it and bought it.

While most of the customers who come by to look at your work will be honest, you may be troubled by a shoplifter. If so, you may not find this out until the end of the day when you have added up your sales and counted your remaining inventory.

If you do suspect someone of intending to steal from your table, watch him or her very carefully until he or she leaves the table. Even if you think he or she might have your item in a pocket, do not accuse or touch the person. If you are absolutely certain that he or she has stolen something from your table, go to the show director or security guard. Be sure to have someone in charge of your display when you leave it.

Another way a customer can cheat you is by claiming that you did not give the correct change. The customer might give you a five dollar bill. You put it away and give him or her the change. He or she counts the change and then claims you owe five dollars because you were given a ten dollar bill. If you have not put the bill in a special place you may not remember what the person did give you and therefore might give the money the customer claims you owe.

The best way to avoid being cheated in this way is to decide on a procedure for taking money and always follow it. When the customer hands you the bill, say out loud what you have been given and how much the customer owes you, for example, "That will be $2.85 out of $5." Also have a specific place to put the bill you are given, temporarily right beside your cash box perhaps. Once the customer accepts the change and walks away, then pick up the bill and put it away in the cash box.

In addition to regular customers at shows you may meet shop managers who are looking for new items to sell in their shops. If you want to sell through shops, give the manager your business card and accept his or hers. If you have a list of the items you sell with the wholesale prices, give the manager a copy. Find out what terms the shop offers and if the shop is willing to buy your items on a wholesale basis. Perhaps the manager will give you an order right away.

If the shop manager asks only to take some of your items on consignment, don't give them to him or her at the show. Instead make an appointment to come to the shop. Once you are there you may decide that this is not a good shop in which to put your items on consignment.

After the Show

When the show is over, pack up all of the unsold items counting how many are left and checking this number against the number brought minus the number sold. To find out how many you sold go through the sales slips you wrote or check the sales list.

Before you forget what happened at the show, write down a few notes. Next year when you hear about the show, look at your notes before deciding whether or not to go. If you go to only a few shows you will not have trouble remembering, but if you go to many, you may forget what happened at each one.

You might want to write your notes on the back of the show announcement that gives information on contacting the director. Note how many of each type of item you sold at the show, what the customers were looking for, and if there were many other crafters selling items like yours. If you are going to the show next year, note where you would like to have your display in case the director lets you have a choice. Keep the sheets about the show together in a folder so that you will be able to find them when you need them.

ELEVEN

Keeping on
the Right Side of the Law—
and of Your Parents

WHETHER you are working alone, with a partner, or with a whole group, you will have to report to an adult authority. By being in business for yourself you have taken on special responsibilities. You are responsible to your parents who in turn are responsible to other people and to the government for you if you are under eighteen. This chapter is one for all of you to read.

If you are working with a sponsor at school you are responsible to that person who in turn is responsible to school authorities for the actions of your group.

Keep Them Informed

Because your parents or advisors are responsible for you, and also because they are interested in you and what you are doing, keep them informed. If they have been in business themselves they will enjoy talking over your problems with you and perhaps helping you to find a solution. If they have never been in business themselves, they may be quite fascinated by what you are doing and enjoy learning with you.

Many problems can be avoided if you get good advice. If your parents or adult leaders know about what you are doing from the beginning, they will be in a much better position to help you. If you know they are behind you, you will have a feeling of self-confidence which makes you better able to solve your own problems.

While you will need the advice and help of adults on certain matters, some decisions are all yours, and you should make them on your own without bothering an adult. If a decision is yours to make, it's to be hoped that your parents or advisors will allow you to make it even though they don't agree with you. If they have given you advice and you have decided not to abide by it, explain what you want to do as kindly as possible so that you will not hurt their feelings.

In other instances, particularly ones that involve a large sum of money or ones in which you might be in personal danger, you should do what you are told to do. It is important to learn to know when you do need help and whom to go to for it.

Much will depend on how big your project is. In most cases it is a good idea to keep adults informed of what you are doing, not so that they will make the decisions for you but rather so that they can warn you of dangers and problems and also occasionally make suggestions on things you might and might not do. If your parents or advisors want to give you advice on your business, listen to what they say and consider the advice carefully. Remember they have had more life experience than you.

Certainly you want your parents to treat your opinions with respect. Do the same with theirs. Talk to them about the big decisions and discuss your plans with them when you take on a big project.

The surest way you will learn is from your own mistakes. Perhaps your mother warned you that it was going to rain and that you'd better be prepared, bringing what you might need to an outdoor show. If it turns out that she was right, it may cost you some display materials and some of your handmade items to learn to listen to the weather forecast before going to a show.

This chapter will try to answer some of the questions you or your parents might have regarding the legal and tax implications of your business. If you have further questions, talk to a lawyer or an accountant who specializes in small businesses or consult a representative from a company like General Business Services (look in the Yellow Pages under "Business Services" or write to General Business Services, 51 Monroe St., Rockville, Md. 20850, for the name of your local representative) that specializes in helping the small businessperson with his or her financial questions.

Child Labor Laws

These laws apply to those under eighteen working as employees, not to young entrepreneurs like yourself who are self-employed.

Income Tax

If you make only a small amount of money you will not need to worry about income tax at all. Whether your sales are only minimal or your business is successful and you start to make quite a bit, keep accurate records so that you know exactly how much you have made and what all of your costs were. Many different costs are deductible from your total sales.

Whether or not you have to fill out and file a federal income tax return (as well as state and local returns in certain localities) depends upon a number of factors, chiefly your total income not only from crafts selling activities but also from summer and part-time jobs, interest on savings accounts, dividends, and the like. It also depends, in part,

---

Tax Form Information

Total Sales for the Year _____

Total Cost of Materials _____

Cost of Equipment _____
   (list items over $100 separately
   with dates of purchase)

Cost of Travel _____
   (number of miles driven, other
   travel costs)

What did you pay others to do jobs
   for you? _____

Rent-costs for the home area used
   for business _____

Legal or professional fees _____

Office supplies and postage _____

Memberships in craft organizations _____

Books and magazine subscriptions _____

Courses _____

Telephone costs _____

Figure 4

upon whether your parents are including you as a dependent on their own tax returns and whether you are a student. It is best to ask your parents' tax advisor, or a local office of the Internal Revenue Service, for specific guidelines. The fact that you may have to file a return does not necessarily mean that you will have to pay a tax. This depends not only upon your total income, but upon what deductions and exclusions are available to you. Again it is best to check with your local office of the Internal Revenue Service. In all events, be sure to keep detailed and accurate records of your sales of products as well as your purchases of materials and supplies, and save all of your receipts and bills. If your parents do their own income tax they will probably do yours if you must file a return. If they hire an accountant or business service representative to do theirs, he or she can do yours also.

In order for anyone to fill out your form you would have to supply them with the information in Figure 4. If you and your parents want to fill out the forms yourself, extensive instructions on filling out federal income tax Form C are in the book *How To Sell Your Art and Crafts* (by Loretta Holz, published by Scribners, 1977).

No matter how much you earn your parents can still claim you as a dependent and get the full exemption for you on their income tax return as long as you are a full-time student for five calendar months of the year and as long as they provided over half of your support for the year.

Social Security

If you do not have a social security number you should apply for one right away. Contact your local office (look in the phone book under U.S. Government) and get an application. The procedure is very simple.

Whether or not you have to pay income tax, you are still required to pay F.I.C.A. or social security tax if your net income from your craft selling (and other self-employment activities) is over $400. As a self-employed person you will have to fill out Form SE and pay a percentage of your earnings (8.1% is the current rate but in 1981 it goes up to 8.35% and in 1986 to 8.5%). If you have a salaried job, your social security taxes on your salary will be paid partly by your employer.

Sales Tax

Does your state have a sales tax? If so you may be responsible to collect it and remit it to the appropriate authorities. The laws differ in each state, so you will have to write for information if you do not know the rules. Most likely you can get a booklet explaining who must collect sales tax and how to collect it by contacting the State Sales Tax Office in your state capital.

If you sell your work through stores you will not be responsible for the sales tax. The store collects the tax and sends in the money; you are not involved at all.

A once-only sale in your home may be treated as a garage sale. People are not required to collect sales tax at their garage sales.

If you take part in shows often, you probably would be required to collect sales tax. The tax booklet will explain how to do this and how to turn in your reports. You may have to send in a quarterly report with the sales tax you have collected. If you are collecting and remitting sales tax on sales of your own crafts, you may be able to avoid having to pay sales tax on the materials which you use for your projects. This too can best be checked by inquiring at your State Sales Tax Office or asking your parents' accountant.

Making Your Business Name Official

To make the name of your business official, register it with the county. This process is easy and inexpensive but you do not have to do it right away. When your business grows and you want to have a special bank account in the name of the business, then it will be necessary.

In order to register your business name call your county clerk's office and ask for information on the procedure. Most likely you will have to fill out a simple form which you obtain from the county clerk's office or from a local stationery store. This form usually must be notarized, that is, it must be marked with the seal of a notary. Someone in the bank where you will open your account can probably help you with this. Then you must pay a small fee in order to register your business name.

Once you apply, the county office will check to be sure you are the only business in the county with this name. If there is another business that already has the name, you must think of a new one. Once your name is officially registered you will get the certificate (called d.b.a. or "doing business as" certificate) that allows you to open a bank account in the name of your business.

Zoning Regulations

Most cities and towns have regulations about the use of each area of the town. If your business is a quiet one and

you don't have heavy customer or truck traffic coming to
your home, then undoubtedly you are not breaking any of
the residential zoning laws.

If your area allows people to run garage sales, you
could run a short craft sale as long as you don't cause so
much noise and disturbance that the neighbors complain
to the police.

You would be in violation of the zoning code, for instance, if you lived in a residential area but were to start a
retail shop that was open year-round and brought much
traffic into the neighborhood. Since this is totally unlikely,
don't worry about violating zoning codes, but instead be
considerate of the neighbors.

Small Claims Court

It's likely you will be dealing with honest people and will
not be cheated. If a shop refuses to pay you for the items
they have accepted and sold, however, you can do something about it. A lawyer would not want the case because
the fee involved would be so small. You can be your own
lawyer!

Most states have a small claims court which is set up to
help people like you who have a small claim against another person or a business. For a small fee you can sue the
company or person for up to a certain maximum amount
of money depending on what your state regulation is. Call
your county courthouse and ask to speak to the clerk of
the small claims court. Ask this person for details on filing
a claim.

But before you take someone to small claims court give
the person or company you will sue the opportunity to
pay you. Telephone several times. Then write a letter
explaining the situation and again request payment. Send

the letter registered mail and keep a copy. Do all of this to show the judge you have done all you could to settle on your own before coming to court.

And remember, your ability to enforce a claim will be only as good as the written records you maintain; when any sale involves a substantial sum of money, you always should get a bill of sale (signed by the buyer) clearly setting forth the items sold, the price, and any other important terms of the sale.

Copyrights

Do you have an original product that sells well because it is unique? You might have spent a long time designing it, looking for the materials, and product-testing it. Perhaps you have wondered if there were any way you could protect your product so that others could not copy it. You may not know that not only books but other types of artistic works can be copyrighted. You can obtain a copyright for the artistic content of your handcrafted item. The procedure is simple.

To copyright your original items you simply put a copyright notice on them. You may do this without contacting the copyright office. The law specifies exactly how this notice must read. You should imprint legibly on the back or base of your work (not on a separate tag or label) the symbol © followed by the year in which the design was created, then followed by your name.

In addition to putting the copyright notice on the item, you can register your copyright for further protection. Registering is not absolutely necessary but it is a good idea because it is a record of when you completed your creation.

To register your copyright write to the Copyright Office, The Library of Congress, Washington, D.C. 20559, and ask for Form G, a very simple form which you will have to fill out in duplicate. You must send two copies of the work you are copyrighting along with the forms and a filing fee. Obviously the copyright office does not want to have its files filled with lovely handmade objects taking up lots of space. Unless your item is small and flat do not send the actual item, but instead send two copies of a photograph of it. You will receive back one copy of your application duly stamped by the copyright office.

On January 1, 1978, the United States Copyright Act was amended to extend the life of new copyrights to a term equal to the remaining life of the creator of the work plus fifty years. If you have copyrighted your product and someone does copy it, you can do something about it. This person probably just does not understand copyrights so you could point out the copyright notice on your item and explain the law to this person. If he or she does not stop copying your item consult with your parents or adult advisor. You can sue the copier to make him stop copying and to recover payments for his use of your design.

On the other hand, be sure that you don't infringe the copyright of another. Check for the copyright notice on items you see. Remember that famous designs like "Snoopy" or the "Sesame Street" characters are copyrighted and you may not copy these designs on items you make. Owners of the "Peanuts" comic strip copyright, for example, have taken craftspeople to court for copying their designs.

Additional Information

A Glossary of Business Terms

amateur—anyone who engages in an activity on a part-time, non-professional basis.

apprentice—someone who is learning a craft under the direction of an experienced craftsperson.

assembly line—an organized way of making a product: usually a number of people each do a small job on each item and pass it along to the next person, sometimes by means of a conveyor belt; you can do this by yourself by working on a group of items, doing one process at a time to the whole group.

booking—an arrangement made by a craftsperson (or anyone selling merchandise) with a private individual who has agreed to have a "party" or demonstration and selling session in his or her home.

capital—the money you need in order to start a business and the money you use to run that business.

classified ad—several lines of type offering to sell something, telling about a sale, etc., included in a newspaper or magazine in a special section where advertisements offering similar items are grouped together by category.

competitor—someone who sells similar items and sells them at the same markets.

consignment—a method of selling your work through a store whereby you leave your items there and the store does not pay you until they are sold; any items not sold will be returned to you.

copyright—legal protection obtained for your artistic creation by marking it with the proper notice (the word, abbreviation, or symbol for copyright, the year, and your name); to register your copyright fill out the correct form in duplicate and send it with two copies or photos of your work plus a small fee to the Copyright Office in Washington, D.C.

crafter—one who does crafts on a part-time basis, usually an amateur.

craftsman (-woman, -person)—one who is involved with one or more crafts on a professional level, often on a full-time basis.

deposit—the partial payment which the customer makes when he or she is putting in a special order.

discount—a reduction from the full amount of the price of an item.

display ad—any advertisement which is not classified; usually it has drawings or photos as well as words.

dividend—a share of the profits made by a company and received by the stockholders.

entrepreneur—one who organizes, operates, and assumes the risks and responsibilities for a business venture.

feature story—an article in a newspaper or magazine which could appear anytime; often it is about a local person, place, or thing.

fliers—circulars or pieces of paper with information printed on them meant for mass distribution.

inventory—all of the items you have made which are ready to sell.

market research—investigation of the sales likely for a certain product.

net income—your total sales minus all of your expenses.

non-profit shop—a store that is run not to make money for the owner but rather for the benefit of those selling through the shop.

overhead—the necessary operating expenses of a business including rent, utilities, insurance, etc.

professional—a person who has competence in a particular field and perhaps earns a living through his or her work in that field.

profit—the money remaining in a business undertaking after all of the costs have been paid.

promotion—anything you do to get attention from the public for your products and your name.

publicity—information presented in such a way that it is noticed by the public.

quality control—checking to be sure that each item which you sell is well made.

retail—selling small quantities to the consumer, usually at full price.

stock—shares in a business; each shareholder owns a certain percentage of the company depending on how many shares he or she has.

venture capital—money which a company or individual will invest in a new company, thereby owning a part of that new company.

wholesale—selling items in larger amounts usually for resale by a retailer; buying usually in large amounts at lower cost.

A List of Non-Profit Shops

Non-profit shops are good places for young people to start selling their work. Here are just some of the non-profit shops that exist all over the country, listed alphabetically by state. If one of these shops is in your area call and ask when you can stop by with samples of your work.

If you want to deal with any of these shops by mail *do not* send samples of your work. Write a brief letter telling about yourself and your craft, explaining what you make and your prices. Enclose with your letter a self-addressed stamped envelope. Wait until you receive a request for samples before sending them.

Little Turtle
6106 Covington Rd.
Fort Wayne, Ind. 46804

Hay Scales Exchange
2 Johnson St.
North Andover, Mass. 01840

Old Town Hall Exchange
Lincoln Center, Mass. 01773

Y.W.C.A. Gallery and Craft Shop
26 Howard St.
Springfield, Mass. 01105

Mulberry Gallery
28 Court St.
Westfield, Mass. 01085

The Women's Exchange
104 North Ave., Box 855
Westfield, N.J. 07090

Craftsmen Unlimited
16 Main St.
Bedford Hills, New York 10507

Consortium
123 E. Water St.
Syracuse, New York 13202

The Sassy Cat
88 N. Main St.
Chagrin Falls, Ohio 44022

Woman's Exchange of Yardley
49 W. Afton Ave.
Yardley, Pa. 19607

Woman's Exchange
88 Racine
Memphis, Tenn. 38111

St. Michael's Woman's Exchange
5 Highland Park Village
Dallas, Texas 75205

Craft Books

If you want to teach yourself a craft there are many good craft books you can use. At your local library check the card catalog under the name of the craft which interests you. If you find a card for a book on the subject, write down the call number of it (perhaps "745," the number of many craft books). Look in the non-fiction section for this book and for other books on the same subject which should be on the same shelf.

The books on the list below are especially recommended. Look in the young readers' room of your library. If you don't find the book you want there, check the adult section because some of these books are for both adults and young readers. If you don't find the book ask the librarian. He or she may be able to get it for you.

Also check at your local book stores for these and other books on crafts. If you will be using the book a lot, you may want to buy your own copy.

Aldrich, Dot. *Creating with Cattails, Cones and Pods.* Great Neck, N.Y.: Hearthside Press, 1971.

Alexander, Marthann. *Simple Weaving.* New York: Tower Publications, 1964.

—— *Weaving on Cardboard.* New York: Taplinger, 1972.

Barber, Janet. *My Learn to Sew Book.* New York: Golden Press, 1970.

Bauzen, Peter and Susanne. *Flower Pressing.* New York: Sterling Publishing, 1972.

Bogen, Constance A. *Beginner's Book of Patchwork, Applique and Quilting.* New York: Dodd, Mead, 1974.

Bucher, Jo. *Complete Guide to Embroidery Stitches and Crewel.* Creative Home Library. New York: Meredith, 1971.

Carlis, John. *How To Make Your Own Greeting Cards.* New York: Watson Guptill, 1968.

Chernoff, Goldie. *Clay Dough, Play Dough.* New York: Walker, 1974.

Clapper, Edna and John. *Pack-O-Fun Treasury of Crafts, Gifts and Toys.* New York: Hawthorn Books, 1971.

Connor, Margaret. *Introducing Fabric Collage.* New York: Watson Guptill, 1969.

Corrigan, Barbara. *I Love to Sew.* Garden City, N.Y.: Doubleday, 1974.

D'Amato, Alex and Janet. *American Indian Craft Inspirations.* New York: M. Evans, 1972.

Eckstein, Artis Aleene. *How to Make Treasures From Trash.* Great Neck, N.Y.: Hearthside Press, 1972.

Grater, Michael. *Paper People.* New York: Taplinger, 1969.

——— *Paper Play.* New York: Taplinger, 1972.

Grunfeld, Frederic, ed. *Games of the World.* New York: Holt, Rinehart & Winston, 1975.

Harwood, Mark. *Fun With Wood.* New York: Grosset & Dunlap, 1975.

Holz, Loretta. *Mobiles You Can Make.* New York: Lothrop, Lee & Shepard, 1975.

——— *Teach Yourself Stitchery.* New York: Lothrop, Lee & Shepard, 1974.

Karasz, Mariska. *Adventures in Stitches.* New York: Funk & Wagnalls, 1975.

Lidstone, John. *Building With Cardboard.* New York: Van Nostrand, 1968.

——— *Building With Wire.* New York: Van Nostrand, 1972.

Lynch, John. *How To Make Mobiles.* New York: Thomas Crowell, 1953.

Martin, Beryl. *Batik For Beginners.* New York: Scribners, 1971.

Meyer, Carolyn. *Miss Patch's Learn To Sew Book.* New York: Harcourt, 1969.

Miller, Irene and Winifred Lubell. *The Stitchery Book.* Garden City, N.Y.: Doubleday, 1965.

Peake, Miriam Morrison. *101 Things To Make For Fun Or Money.* New York: Scholastic Book Services, 1964.

Petersen, Grete. *Making Toys With Plywood.* New York: Reinhold, 1967.

Pflug, Betsy. *You Can.* New York: Van Nostrand, 1969.

Plummer, Beverly. *Earth Presents: How To Make Beautiful Gifts From Nature's Bounty.* New York: Atheneum, 1974.

Schegger, T. M. *Make Your Own Mobiles.* New York: Sterling Publishing, 1965.

Schulz, Walter. *Toys For Fun and How To Make Them.* Milwaukee: Bruce Publishing, 1966.

Sommer, Elyse. *Contemporary Costume Jewelry: A Multi Media Approach.* New York: Crown, 1974.

Sommer, Elyse with Joellen Sommer. *A Patchwork Applique & Quilting Primer.* New York: Lothrop, Lee & Shepard, 1975.

———— *Sew Your Own Accessories.* New York: Lothrop, Lee & Shepard, 1972.

Stephan, Barbara B. *Creating With Tissue Paper.* New York: Crown, 1973.

Temko, Florence. *Decoupage Crafts.* Garden City, N.Y.: Doubleday, 1976.

———— *Paper—Folded, Cut, Sculpted.* New York: Macmillan, 1974.

Tyler, Mabs. *The Big Book of Soft Toys.* New York: McGraw-Hill, 1972.

Villiard, Paul. *Jewelry Making.* Garden City, N.Y.: Doubleday, 1973.

Waltner, Willard and Elma. *Hobbycraft Toys and Games.* New York: Lantern Press, 1965.

———— *The New Hobby Craft Book.* New York: Lantern Press, 1963.

Weiss, Peter. *Simple Printmaking.* New York: Lothrop, Lee & Shepard, 1976.

Wilson, Erica. *Fun With Crewel Embroidery.* New York: Scribners, 1965.

Wright, Lois. *Weathered Wood Craft.* New York: Lothrop, Lee & Shepard, 1973.

Zechlin, Katherina. *Games You Can Build Yourself.* New York: Sterling Publishing, 1975.

Sources of Craft Show News

If you want to participate in art and craft shows, flea markets, and similar events you must know about them in advance. One way to find out is to subscribe to one of the following magazines which list shows. Some of these publications are entirely made up of the listings while others have listings as only part of the magazine.

After each magazine, in parenthesis, is the area of the country the publication covers. If nothing appears in parenthesis, the show listing is nationwide. If you are interested in a certain magazine, write requesting the cost of a sample copy and a subscription.

Colorado Art Show News (Colorado and adjoining states)
P.O. Box 609
Littleton, Colo. 80120

Frank Cox (Florida and Georgia)
3980 8th Ave. #309
San Diego, Calif. 92103

Craft Connection (Midwest)
Publication of the Minnesota Crafts Council
Tom Barry, Subscriptions
900 Fairmount Ave.
St. Paul, Minn. 55105

Craft Dimensions Artisanales (Canada)
Canadian Guild of Crafts
29 Prince Arthur Ave.
Toronto, Ontario M5R1B2 Canada

Craft Horizons
American Crafts Council
44 West 53rd St.
New York, N.Y. 10019

Crafts Fair Guide (Northern California)
Box 9132
Berkeley, Calif. 94709

The Crafts Report
116 University Place
New York, N.Y. 10003

Creative Crafts
Box 700
Newton, N.J. 07860

Decorating and Craft Ideas
1303 Foch St.
Fort Worth, Texas 76107

Festival USA
Superintendent of Documents
U.S. Government Printing Office
Washington, D.C. 20402

The Goodfellow Review of Crafts (nationwide but strongest in
California)
P.O. Box 4520
Berkeley, Calif. 94704

Handcrafters' News
808 High Mountain Rd.
Franklin Lakes, N.J. 07417

Highland Highlights (Southern Appalachians area)
Southern Highland Handcraft Guild
15 Reddick Road
Asheville, N.C. 28805

Mid-West Art (Midwest)
Gary Pisarek, Publisher
2025 E. Fernwood Ave.
P.O. Box 4419
Milwaukee, Wis. 53207

Midwest Art Fare (Upper Midwest)
Bill Jacobsen
Box 195
Garrison, Iowa 52229

National Calendar of Indoor/Outdoor Art Fairs
National Calendar of Open Art Exhibits
Henry Niles
5423 New Haven Ave.
Fort Wayne, Ind. 46803

Near North News (Chicago area and some surrounding states)
Sylvia Zappa, Managing Editor
26 E. Huron
Chicago, Ill. 60611

New York State Craftsmen/Bulletin (New York)
P.O. Box 733
Ithaca, N.Y. 14850

Ozark Mountaineer (Ozark Mountains area)
Clay Anderson, Editor
Branson, Mo. 65616

Regional Art Fair List (Upper Midwest)
Nelson Brown
Box 136, Rt. #1
Stockholm, Wis. 54769

Scan (Southern Crafts and Arts News) (mainly Southeast)
Jere Aldridge, Editor and Publisher
Route 14, Box 571
Cullman, Ala. 35055

Sunshine Artists
Stan Bianco
Sun Country Enterprises, Inc.
Drawer 836
Fern Park, Fla. 32730

Tri-State Trader (Midwest)
Thomas Mayhill, Editor and Publisher
P.O. Box 90
Knightstown, Ind. 46148

Westart (West Coast)
Bud Pisarek, Publisher
P.O. Box 1396
Auburn, Calif. 95603

The Working Craftsman
(formerly Craft/Midwest)
Marilyn Heise, Editor
Box 42
Northbrook, Ill. 60062

Index

141